Mathematics and Music

MATHEMATICAL WORLD   VOLUME 28

Mathematics and Music

David Wright

AMS
AMERICAN MATHEMATICAL SOCIETY
www.ams.org
Providence, Rhode Island

2000 *Mathematics Subject Classification.* Primary 00–01, 00A06.

For additional information and updates on this book, visit
www.ams.org/bookpages/mawrld-28

Library of Congress Cataloging-in-Publication Data
Wright, David, 1949–
   Mathematics and music / David Wright.
     p. cm. — (Mathematical world ; v. 28)
   Includes bibliographical references and index.
   ISBN 978-0-8218-4873-9 (alk. paper)
   1. Musical intervals and scales.   2. Music theory—Mathematics.   I. Title.

ML3809.W85   2009
781.01′51—dc22

                                                          2009014813

About the Author

David Wright is professor of mathematics at Washington University in St. Louis, where he currently serves as Chair of the Mathematics Department. He received his Ph.D. in Mathematics from Columbia University, New York City. A leading researcher in the fields of affine algebraic geometry and polynomial automorphisms, he has produced landmark publications in these areas and has been an invited speaker at numerous international mathematics conferences. He designed and teaches a university course in Mathematics and Music, the notes from which formed the beginnings of this book.

As a musician, David is an arranger and composer of vocal music, where his work often integrates the close harmony style called barbershop harmony with jazz, blues, gospel, country, doo-wop, and contemporary a cappella. He is Associate Director of the St. Charles Ambassadors of Harmony, an award winning male chorus of 160 singers. He also serves as a musical consultant and arranger for numerous other vocal ensembles. He is active in the Barbershop Harmony Society and was inducted into its Hall of Fame in 2008. As arranger and music historian David has been featured in national radio and TV broadcasts at home and abroad and has authored several articles on vocal harmony.

Contents

Introduction

The author's perspective. Mathematics and music are both lifelong passions for me. For years they appeared to be independent non-intersecting interests; one did not lead me to the other, and there seemed to be no obvious use of one discipline in the application of the other. Over the years, however, I slowly came to understand that there is, at the very least, a positive, supportive coexistence between mathematics and music in my own thought processes, and that in some subtle way I was appealing to skills and instincts endemic to one subject when actively engaged with the other. In this way the relationship between mathematical reasoning and musical creativity, and the way humans grasp and appreciate both subjects, became a matter of interest that eventually resulted in a college course called Mathematics and Music, first offered in the spring of 2002 at Washington University in St. Louis, the notes of which have evolved into this book.

It has been observed that mathematics is the most abstract of the sciences, music the most abstract of the arts. Mathematics attempts to understand conceptual and logical truth and appreciates the intrinsic beauty of such. Music evokes mood and emotion by the audio medium of tones and rhythms without appealing to circumstantial means of eliciting such innate human reactions. Therefore it is not surprising that the symbiosis of the two disciplines is an age-old story. The Greek mathematician Pythagoras noted the integral relationships between frequencies of musical tones in a consonant interval; the 18th century musician J. S. Bach studied the mathematical problem of finding a practical way to tune keyboard instruments. In today's world it is not at all unusual to encounter individuals who have at least some interest in both subjects.

However, it is sometimes the case that a person with an inclination for one of these disciplines views the other with some apprehension: a mathematically inclined person may regard music with admiration but as something beyond his/her reach. Reciprocally, the musically inclined often view mathematics with a combination of fear and disdain, believing it to be unrelated to the artistic nature of a musician. Perhaps, then, it is my personal mission to attempt to remove this barrier for others, since it has never existed for me, being one who roams freely and comfortably in both worlds, going back and forth between the right and left sides of the brain with no hesitation. Thus I have come to value the ability to bring to bear the whole capacity of the mind when working in *any* creative endeavor.

Purpose of this book. This short treatise is intended to serve as a text for a freshman level college course that, among other things, addresses the issues mentioned above. The book investigates interrelationships between mathematics and music. It reviews some background concepts in both subjects as they are encountered. Along the way, the reader will hopefully augment his/her knowledge of both mathematics and music. The two will be discussed and developed side by side, their languages intermingled and unified, with the goal of breaking down the dyslexia that inhibits their mental amalgamation and encouraging the analytic, quantitative, artistic, and emotional aspects of the mind to work together in the creative process. Musical and mathematical notions are brought together, such as scales/modular arithmetic, octave identification/equivalence relation, intervals/logarithms, equal temperament/exponents, overtones/integers, tone/trigonometry, timbre/harmonic analysis, tuning/rationality. When possible, discussions of musical and mathematical notions are directly interwoven. Occasionally the discourse dwells for a while on one subject and not the other, but eventually the connection is brought to bear. Thus you will find in this treatise an integrative treatment of the two subjects.

Music concepts covered include diatonic and chromatic scales (standard and non-standard), intervals, rhythm, meter, form, melody, chords, progressions, octave equivalence, overtones, timbre, formants, equal temperament, and alternate methods of tuning. Mathematical concepts covered include integers, rational and real numbers, equivalence relations, geometric transformations, groups, rings, modular arithmetic, unique factorization, logarithms, exponentials, and periodic functions. Each of these notions enters the scene because it is involved in one way or another with a point where mathematics and music converge.

The book does not presume much background in either mathematics or music. It assumes high-school level familiarity with algebra, trigonometry, functions, and graphs. It is hoped the student has had some exposure to musical staffs, standard clefs, and key signatures, though all of these are explained in the text. Some calculus enters the picture in Chapter 10, but it is explained from first principles in an intuitive and non-rigorous way.

What is not in this book. Lots. It should be stated up front, and emphasized, that the intent of this book is *not* to teach how to create music using mathematics, nor vice versa. Also it does not seek out connections which are obscure or esoteric, possibly excepting the cursory excursion into serial music (the rationale for which, at least in part, is to ponder the arbitrariness of the twelve-tone chromatic scale). Rather, it explores the foundational commonalities between the two subjects. Connections that seem (to the author) to be distant or arguable, such as the golden ratio, are omitted or given only perfunctory mention.

Yet it should be acknowledged that there is quite a bit of material in line with the book's purpose which is not included. Much more could be said, for example, about polyrhythm, harmony, voicing, form, formants of musical instruments and human vowels, and systems of tuning. And of course there is much more that could be included if calculus were a prerequisite, such as a much deeper discussion of harmonic analysis. Also missing are the many wonderful connections between mathematics and music that could be established, and examples that could be used, involving non-Western music (scales, tuning, form, etc.). This omission owes itself to the author's inexperience in this most fascinating realm.

Overview of the chapters. The book is organized as follows:

- Chapter 1 lays out the basic mathematical and musical concepts which will be needed throughout the course: sets, equivalence relations, functions and graphs, integers, rational numbers, real numbers, pitch, clefs, notes, musical intervals, scales, and key signatures.

- Chapter 2 deals with the horizontal structure of music: note values and time signatures, as well as overall form.

- Chapter 3 discusses the vertical structure of music: chords, conventional harmony, and the numerology of chord identification.

- Musical intervals are explained as mathematical ratios in Chapter 4, and the standard keyboard intervals are introduced in this language.

- Chapter 5 lays out the mathematical underpinnings for additive measurement of musical intervals, relating this to logarithms and exponentials.

- Equal temperament (standard and non-standard) is the topic of Chapter 6, which also gives a brief introduction to twelve-tone music.

- The mathematical foundations of modular arithmetic and its relevance to music are presented in Chapter 7. This involves some basic abstract algebra, which is developed from first principles without assuming any prior knowledge of the subject.

- Chapter 8 delves further into abstract algebra, deriving properties of the integers, such as unique factorization, which are the underpinnings of certain musical phenomena.

- Chapter 9 gives a precursor of harmonics by interpreting positive integers as musical intervals and finding keyboard approximations of such intervals.

- The subject of harmonics is developed further in Chapter 10, which relates timbre to harmonics and introduces some relevant calculus concepts, giving a brief, non-rigorous introduction to continuity, periodic functions, and the basic theorem of harmonic analysis.

- Chapter 11 covers rational numbers and rational, or "just", intervals. It presents certain classical "commas", and how they arise, and it discusses some of the basic just intervals, such as the greater whole tone and the just major third. It also explains why all intervals except multi-octaves in any equal tempered scale are irrational.

- Finally, Chapter 12 describes various alternative systems of tuning that have been used which are designed to give just renditions of certain intervals. Some benefits and drawbacks of each are discussed.

Suggestions for the course. This book is meant for a one-semester course open to college students at any level. Such a course could be cross-listed as an offering in both the mathematics and music departments so as to satisfy curriculum requirements in either field. It could also be structured to fulfill a quantitative requirement in liberal arts. Since the material interrelates with and complements subjects such as calculus, music theory, and physics of sound, it could be a part of an interdisciplinary "course cluster" offered by some universities.

The course will need no formal prerequisites. Beyond the high-school level all mathematical and musical concepts are explained and developed from the ground up. As such the course will be attractive not only to students who have interests in both subjects, but also to those who are fluent with one and desire knowledge of the other, as well as to those who are familiar with neither. Thus the course can be expected to attract students at all levels of college (even graduate students), representing a wide range of majors. Accordingly, the course must accommodate the different sets of backgrounds, and the instructor must be particularly sensitive to the fact that certain material is a review to some in the class while being new to others, and that, depending on the topic, those subgroups of students can vary, even interchange. More than the usual amount of care should be taken to include all the students all the time.

Of course, the topics in the book can be used selectively, rearranged, and/or augmented at the instructor's discretion. The instructor who finds it impossible to cover all the topics in a single semester or quarter could possibly omit some of the abstract algebra in Chapters 7 and 8. However it is not advisable to avoid abstract mathematical concepts, as this is an important part of this integrative approach.

Viewing, listening to, and discussing musical examples will be an important part of the class, so the classroom should be equipped with a high-quality sound system, computer hookup, and a keyboard.

Some goals of the course are as follows:

- To explore relationships between mathematics and music.

- To develop and enhance the students' musical knowledge and creativity.

- To develop and enhance the students' skills in some basic mathematical topics and in abstract reasoning.

- To integrate the students' artistic and analytic skills.

- (if equipment is available) To introduce the computer and synthesizer as interactive tools for musical and mathematical creativity.

Regarding the last item, my suggestion is that students be given access to some computer stations that have a notation/playback software such as Finale and that the students receive some basic instruction in how to enter notes and produce playback. It is also helpful if the computer is connected via a MIDI (Musical Instrument Digital Interface) device to a tunable keyboard synthesizer, in which case the student also needs to have some instruction in how the software drives the synthesizer.

Some of the homework assignments should ask for a short composition which demonstrates a specific property or principle discussed in the course, such as a particular form, melodic symmetry, or the twelve-tone technique, which might then be turned in as a sound file along with a score and possibly an essay discussing what was done.

The course can be enhanced by a few special guest lecturers, such as a physicist who can demonstrate and discuss the acoustics of musical instruments, or a medical doctor who can explain the mechanism of the human ear. It can be quite educational and enjoyable if the entire group of students are able to attend one or more musical performances together, e.g., a symphony orchestra, a string quartet, an *a cappella* vocal ensemble, ragtime, modern jazz. This can be integrated in various ways with a number of topics in the course, such as modes, scales, form, rhythm, harmony, intonation, and timbre. The performance might be ensued in the classroom by a discussion of the role played by these various musical components, or even an analysis of some piece performed.

There is only a brief bibliography, consisting of books on my shelf which aided me in writing this book. I recommend all these sources as supplements. A lengthy bibliography on mathematics and music can be found in David J. Benson's grand treatise *Music: A Mathematical Offering* [2], which gives far more technical and in-depth coverage of nearly all the topics addressed here, plus more; it could be used as a textbook for a sequel to the course for which the present book is intended.

Acknowledgements. I want to thank Edward Dunne, Senior Editor at the American Mathematical Society, for providing the initial impetus for this project by encouraging me to forge my course notes into a book, and carefully reading the first draft. I also thank two of my colleagues in the Department of Mathematics at Washington University, Professors Guido Weiss and Victor Wickerhauser, for some assistance with Chapter 10.

This book was typeset by LATEX using TEXShop. The music examples were created with MusiXTEX and the figures with MetaPost.

DAVID WRIGHT
PROFESSOR AND CHAIR
DEPARTMENT OF MATHEMATICS
WASHINGTON UNIVERSITY IN ST. LOUIS
ST. LOUIS, MO 63130

Chapter 1

Basic Mathematical and Musical Concepts

Sets and Numbers. We assume familiarity with the basic notions of set theory, such as the concepts of *element* of a set, *subset* of a set, *union* and *intersection* of sets, and *function* from one set to another. We assume familiarity with the descriptors *one-to-one* and *onto* for a function.

Following standard convention, we will denote by $\mathbb{R}$ the set of *real numbers,* by $\mathbb{Q}$ the set of *rational numbers,* and by $\mathbb{Z}$ the set of *integers.* These sets have an ordering, and we will assume familiarity with the symbols $<, \leq, >, \geq$ and basic properties such as: If $a, b, c \in \mathbb{R}$ with $a < b$ and $c > 0$, then $ac < bc$; if $a, b, c \in \mathbb{R}$ with $a < b$ and $c < 0$, then $ac > bc$. We will write $\mathbb{R}^+$ for the set of positive real numbers, $\mathbb{Q}^+$ for the set of positive rational numbers, and $\mathbb{Z}^+$ for the set of positive integers:

$$\mathbb{R}^+ = \{x \in \mathbb{R} \mid x > 0\}$$
$$\mathbb{Q}^+ = \{x \in \mathbb{Q} \mid x > 0\}$$
$$\mathbb{Z}^+ = \{x \in \mathbb{Z} \mid x > 0\}.$$

The set $\mathbb{Z}^+$ is sometimes called the set of *natural numbers,* also denoted $\mathbb{N}$.

Some Properties of Integers. Given $m, n \in \mathbb{Z}$, we say "m divides n", and write $m|n$, if there exists $q \in \mathbb{Z}$ such that $n = qm$. Grade school arithmetic teaches that for any positive integers m and n, we can divide n by m to get a remainder r having the property $0 \leq r < m$. For example, in the case $m = 9$ and $n = 123$, we have $123 = 13 \cdot 9 + 6$, so $r = 6$. This principle generalizes in the following algorithm to the case where n is any integer.

DIVISION ALGORITHM. *Given $m \in \mathbb{Z}^+$ and $n \in \mathbb{Z}$, there exist $q, r \in \mathbb{Z}$ with $0 \leq r < m$ such that $n = qm + r$.*

We will occasionally appeal to one of the axioms of mathematics called the Well-Ordering Principle, which states:

WELL-ORDERING PRINCIPLE. *Any non-empty subset of $\mathbb{Z}^+$ has a smallest element.*

This assertion looks innocent, but cannot be proved without some other similar assumption, so it is taken as an axiom.

Intervals of Real Numbers. We will employ the following standard notation for *intervals* in $\mathbb{R}$: for $a, b \in \mathbb{R}$,

$$(a, b) = \{x \in \mathbb{R} \mid a < x < b\}$$
$$[a, b] = \{x \in \mathbb{Z} \mid a \leq x \leq b\}.$$

Similarly, we write $(a, b]$ and $[a, b)$ for the half-open intervals.

Functions and Graphs. A function from some subset of $\mathbb{R}$ into $\mathbb{R}$ has a *graph,* and we assume familiarity with this notion, as well as the terms *domain* and *range.* We will often use the standard conventions which express a function as $y = f(x)$, where x is the independent variable and y is the dependent variable. When the independent variable parameterizes time, we sometimes denote it by t, so that the function is written $y = f(t)$. A familiar example is $y = mx + b$, where $m, b \in \mathbb{R}$, whose graph is a straight line having slope m and y-intercept b. Another is the function $y = x^2$, whose graph is a parabola with vertex at the origin.

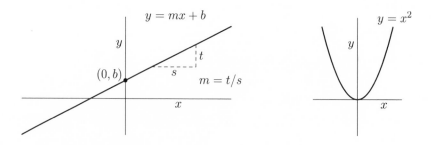

Two functions which will be especially relevant to our topic are the trigonometric functions $y = \sin x$ and $y = \cos x$.

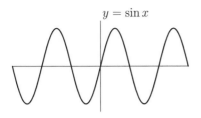

$y = \sin x$

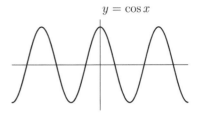

$y = \cos x$

Transformations of Graphs. We will need to understand some procedures, called geometric transformations, which move and deform a graph in certain ways. Let $c \in \mathbb{R}$.

(1) <u>Vertical shift</u>: The graph of $y = f(x) + c$ is obtained by shifting the graph of $y = f(x)$ upward by a distance of c.

(2) <u>Horizontal shift</u>: The graph $y = f(x - c)$ is obtained by shifting the graph of $y = f(x)$ to the right by a distance of c.

(3) <u>Vertical stretch</u>: The graph of $y = cf(x)$ is obtained by stretching the graph of $y = f(x)$ vertically by a factor of c.

(4) <u>Horizontal stretch</u>: The graph of $y = f(x/c)$ is obtained by stretching the graph of $y = f(x)$ horizontally by a factor of c. (Here we assume $c \neq 0$.)

If c in (1) or (2) is a negative number, we must understand that shifting upward (respectively, to the right) by c actually means shifting downward (respectively, to the left) by a distance of $|c| = -c$. If $0 < c < 1$ in (3) or (4) the stretchings are compressions, and if $c < 0$ the stretchings entail a flip about the x-axis in (3), the y-axis in (4).

Below are graphs which illustrate some of these transformations for the function $y = x^2$:

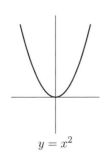

$y = x^2$

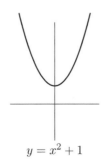

$y = x^2 + 1$

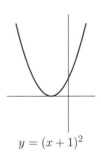

$y = (x + 1)^2$

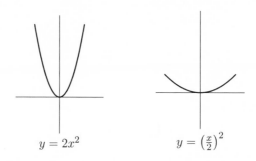

$$y = 2x^2 \qquad\qquad y = \left(\tfrac{x}{2}\right)^2$$

Equivalence Relations. Let S be a set and let $\sim$ be a relationship which holds between certain pairs of elements. If the relationship holds between s and t we write $s \sim t$. For example, S could be a set of solid-colored objects and $s \sim t$ could be the relationship "s is the same color as t". We say that $\sim$ is an *equivalence relation* if the following three properties hold for all $s, t, u \in S$:

(1) $s \sim s$ (reflexivity)

(2) If $s \sim t$, then $t \sim s$ (symmetry)

(3) If $s \sim t$ and $t \sim u$, then $s \sim u$ (transitivity)

When these hold, we define the *equivalence class* of $s \in S$ to be the set $\{t \in S \mid t \sim s\}$. The equivalence classes form a *partition* of S, meaning that S is the disjoint union of the equivalence classes.

Pitch. A musical tone is the result of a regular vibration transmitted through the air as a sound wave. The *pitch* of the tone is the frequency of the vibration. Frequency is usually measured in cycles per second, or *hertz* (after the German physicist Heinrich Hertz (1857-1894)), which is abbreviated *Hz*. For example, standard tuning places the note A above middle C on a musical staff at 440 Hz. It is notated on the treble clef as:

The range of audibility for the human ear is about 20 Hz to 20,000 Hz. We will, however, associate a positive real number x with the frequency x Hz, so that the set of pitches is in one-to-one correspondence with the set $\mathbb{R}^+$.

Notes. In a musical score, specific pitches are called for in a musical score by notes on a staff. We assume familiarity with the usual bass and treble

clefs

Middle C as it appears on the treble and bass clefs

and the labeling of notes on the lines and spaces of those clefs using the letters A through G. These notes are arranged as follows on a keyboard instrument.

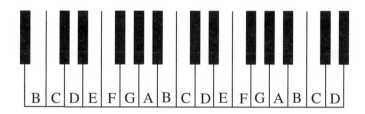

Note the presence of "white notes" and "black notes" and the pattern of their juxtapositions.

Abstractly, we can envision a keyboard which extends infinitely (and beyond the range of audibility) in both directions, giving an infinite set of notes. This infinite set does not represent all pitches, as there are pitches between adjacent notes. We refer to those notes that appear on the extended keyboard as *keyboard notes.*

We will be needing a concise way to refer to specific keyboard notes, hence we will employ the following standard convention: The note C which lies four octaves below middle C is denoted C_0. This note is below the range of the piano keyboard. For any integer n, the C which lies n octaves above C_0 (below C_0 when n is negative) is denoted C_n. Hence middle C is C_4, the C below middle C is C_3, and the lowest C on the piano keyboard is C_1. The other notes will be identified by the integer corresponding to the highest C below that note.

The other notes will be identified by the following procedure: First, strip away any sharp or flat alteration, and find the highest C which is lower than or equal to that note. The original note gets the subscript of that C. Hence the $F^\sharp$ below C_4 is $F_3^\sharp$, while the $F^\sharp$ above C_4 is $F_4^\sharp$. The lowest $B^\flat$ on the piano keyboard is $B_0^\flat$, and the $B^\flat$ in the middle of the treble clef is $B_4^\flat$. Note also that $B_3^\sharp$ and $C_4^\flat$ both coincide with C_4.

Musical Intervals. The *interval* between two notes can be thought of informally as the "distance" between their two associated pitches. (This is to be distinguished from the use of the term "interval" in mathematics for a subset of $\mathbb{R}$ of the type $[a, b]$.) The piano is tuned using *equal temperament* (to be discussed later in detail), which means that the interval between any two adjacent keys (white or black) is the same. This interval is called a *semitone*. The interval of two semitones is a *step*, or *major second*, hence a semitone is a *half-step*, sometimes called a *minor second*. An octave is 12 semitones. Here is a list giving common nomenclature for various intervals:

half-step, or *minor second* (1 semitone)
step, major second, or *whole tone* (2 semitones)
minor third (3 semitones)
major third (4 semitones)
fourth, or *perfect fourth* (5 semitones)
tritone (6 semitones)
fifth, or *perfect fifth* (7 semitones)
minor sixth, or *augmented fifth* (8 semitones)
major sixth (9 semitones)
minor seventh, or *augmented sixth* (10 semitones)
major seventh (11 semitones)
octave (12 semitones)
minor ninth (13 semitones)
ninth (14 semitones)

The meaning of the term "interval" will be made mathematically precise later, but for now we will speak in terms of steps, half-steps, fourths, octaves, etc. Also, we will later discuss small modifications of these intervals (e.g., *just* and *Pythagorean* intervals), so to avoid confusion we sometimes refer to the intervals between notes on the abstract infinite keyboard as *keyboard* intervals, or *tempered* intervals. For example we will introduce the Pythagorean major third, which is greater than the keyboard's major third.

We call intervals positive or negative according to whether they are upward or downward, respectively. We sometimes indicate this by using the terms "upward" and "downward" or by using the terms "positive" and "negative" (or "plus" and "minus"). The interval from C_4 to E_3 could be described as down a minor sixth, or as negative a minor sixth.

Octave Equivalence. Music notation and terminology often takes a view which identifies notes that are octaves apart. In this scenario there are only twelve notes on the piano, and "A" refers to any note A, not distinguishing between, say, A_5 and A_1. This is nothing more than a relationship on the set of notes in the chromatic scale: Two notes will be related if the interval between them is n octaves, for some integer n. One easily verifies that the three properties reflexivity, symmetry, and transitivity are satisfied, so that this is in fact an equivalence relation. We will use the term "modulo octave" in reference to this equivalence relation; hence, for example, $B_2^\flat$ and $B_5^\flat$ are equivalent, modulo octave. A note which is identified by a letter with no subscript can be viewed as an equivalence class by this equivalence relation. Thus $B^\flat$ can be viewed as the equivalence class of all notes $B_n^\flat$, where $n \in \mathbb{Z}$. We will call the equivalence classes of this equivalence relation *note classes*.

This equivalence of octave identification is similarly applied to intervals: the intervals of a whole-step and a ninth, for example, are equivalent, modulo octave. Each equivalence class of intervals has a unique representative which is positive and strictly less than an octave. (Since intervals are often measured in semitones or steps, this harkens to the mathematical concept of modular arithmetic, and later we will make that connection precise.)

In the ensuing discussion of scales and keys we will adopt the perspective of octave identification.

Accidentals. Notes can be altered by the use of sharps and flats. A sharp $\sharp$ placed immediately before a note on the staff raises its pitch by a semitone, a flat $\flat$ lowers it a semitone, and a natural $\natural$ cancels the effect of a sharp or a flat. Music notation also sometimes employs the double sharp $\times$ and the double flat $\flat\flat$, which alter the pitch two semitones. We denote the class of such an altered note by writing the sharp or flat as a superscript, as in $D^\sharp$ or $A^\flat$. These altering devices are called *accidentals*. Note then that $F^\sharp$ is the same note class as $G^\flat$ and that $C_5^\flat$ is the same note as B_4. When two notes give the same pitch in this way we say they are *enharmonically* equivalent. (This gives rise to an equivalence class on notes.)

Scales. The standard scale, based on C, is the sequence of ascending notes C D E F G A B C. Since we are using octave equivalence, the last scale note C is redundant; the scale is determined by the sequence C D E F G A B. These are the white keys on the keyboard. The whole-step and half-step intervals (modulo octave) between the successive scale notes are:

$$ C \xrightarrow{1} D \xrightarrow{1} E \xrightarrow{1/2} F \xrightarrow{1} G \xrightarrow{1} A \xrightarrow{1} B \xrightarrow{1/2} C $$

This sequence $1, 1, \frac{1}{2}, 1, 1, 1, \frac{1}{2}$ of whole-step and half-step intervals initiating with C is incorporated in musical notation, making C the "default" key. One has to be aware of this convention, as there is nothing in the notation itself to indicate that the distance from, say, E to F is a half-step whereas the distance between F and G is a whole-step. The above scale can be represented on the treble clef, starting with C_4 (middle C), as:

We will say that two sequences of pitches are equivalent if the sequence of respective intervals is the same. Note, for example, that the scale contains the two equivalent *tetrachords* (i.e., four note sequences bounded by the interval of a perfect fourth) CDEF and GABC.

Key Signatures. For the moment we will call any sequence of eight consecutive notes a *standard scale* if it is equivalent to the C scale. Note that the sequence $E^\flat$ F G $A^\flat$ $B^\flat$ C D $E^\flat$ is a standard scale.

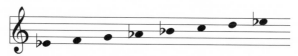

One verifies easily that any ascending sequence of eight consecutive white notes that makes a standard scale must be a C to C sequence. To get a standard scale beginning and ending with a note other than C requires using black notes. The scales F to F and G to G require only one black note. If B is replaced by $B^\flat$, then the F to F scale

$$F \xrightarrow{1} G \xrightarrow{1} A \xrightarrow{1/2} B^\flat \xrightarrow{1} C \xrightarrow{1} D \xrightarrow{1} E \xrightarrow{1/2} F$$

becomes equivalent to the C to C scale, and hence is a standard scale. Similarly if F is replaced by $F^\sharp$, the G to G scale

$$G \xrightarrow{1} A \xrightarrow{1} B \xrightarrow{1/2} C \xrightarrow{1} D \xrightarrow{1} E \xrightarrow{1} F^\sharp \xrightarrow{1/2} G$$

becomes a standard scale. This explains the key signatures for the major keys of F and G:

A key signature merely "tailors" notes so as to effect the standard scale in the desired key.

More generally, flatting the seventh note of *any* standard scale induces a new standard scale based on the fourth note of the original scale. Hence replacing E by $E^\flat$ in the F to F scale yields the $B^\flat$ to $B^\flat$ scale

$$B^\flat \xrightarrow{1} C \xrightarrow{1} D \xrightarrow{1/2} E^\flat \xrightarrow{1} F \xrightarrow{1} G \xrightarrow{1} A \xrightarrow{1/2} B^\flat$$

Hence the key signature of $B^\flat$ is:

Continuing this gives us a sequence of keys C, F, $B^\flat$, $E^\flat$, $A^\flat$, $D^\flat$, $G^\flat$, $C^\flat$. (This sequence continues in theory, but subsequent key signatures will require double flats and eventually other multiple flats.) These are shown below, with the proper placement of flats on the bass and treble clefs.

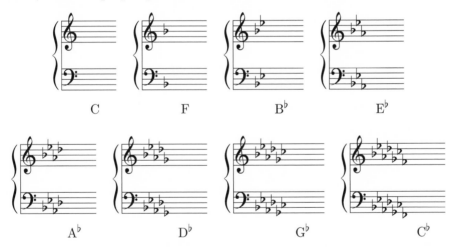

Note that each successive keynote lies the interval of a fourth (5 semitones) above the previous. Since we are identifying notes an octave apart, it is also correct to say that each successive keynote lies a fifth (7 semitones) below the previous one.

Similarly, sharping the fourth note of any standard scale induces a new standard scale based on the fifth note of the original scale, leading to the sequence of keys C, G, D, A, E, B, F$^\sharp$, C$^\sharp$, shown below.

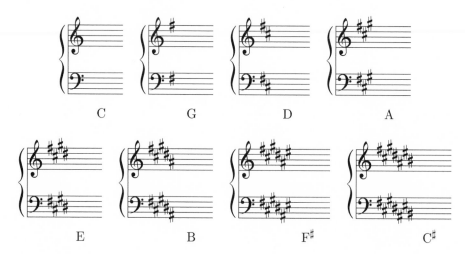

Notice that the two sequences of key signatures, those using flats and those using sharps, wrap against each other, yielding three pairs of keys that are enharmonically equivalent: D$^\flat \sim$ C$^\sharp$, G$^\flat \sim$ F$^\sharp$, and C$^\flat \sim$ B.

Diatonic and Chromatic Notes. The standard scale is called the *diatonic* scale, whereas the scale containing all the notes is called the *chromatic* scale. Note that the chromatic scale has twelve notes, modulo octave, as opposed to the diatonic scale's seven notes, modulo octave. In a given key, those notes that lie within the diatonic scale are called *diatonic notes*. They form a subset of the set of notes of the chromatic scale. (In fact, a scale can be defined as a subsequence of the sequence of chromatic scale notes.)

Cyclic Permutations. Given a finite sequence $x_1, x_2, \ldots, x_n$ of elements in any set, a *cyclic permutation* of this set is obtained by choosing an integer i with $1 \leq i \leq n$, removing entries $x_1, \ldots, x_i$ from the beginning of the sequence and inserting them in order at the end, so as to obtain the sequence

$$x_{i+1}, x_{i+2}, \ldots, x_n, x_1, x_2, \ldots, x_i.$$

If we were to arrange the sequence $x_1, x_2, \ldots, x_n$ on a clock with n positions, say, in clockwise fashion with x_1 at the top, then rotate by i positions in the clockwise direction, this cyclic permutation would be obtained by reading off the elements in clockwise fashion, starting from the top. If we chose $i = n$ we would get the original sequence, so that any finite sequence is a cyclic permutation of itself. The cyclic permutations corresponding to the integers $i = 1, \ldots, n - 1$ are called the *non-trivial cyclic permutations* of $x_1, x_2, \ldots, x_n$.

For example, consider the sequence of numbers $7, 4, 1, 7$. Its cyclic permutations are the sequences $4, 1, 7, 7$, $1, 7, 7, 4$, $7, 7, 4, 1$, and $7, 4, 1, 7$, the first three being the non-trivial ones.

Note that it is possible for a sequence to be a non-trivial cyclic permutation of itself. For example, if we permute the sequence $3, 5, 3, 3, 5, 3$ using $i = 3$, we get the same sequence.

Modality and Key. We have designated the standard scale, in a given key, as a sequence of notes: in C it is the sequence C D E F G A B C. As we pointed out, the last note is redundant, since we are using octave equivalence, so the scale is given by the 7-entry sequence C D E F G A B, and this determines the sequence of adjacent intervals $1, 1, \frac{1}{2}, 1, 1, 1, \frac{1}{2}$ (which still has 7 entries). Consider now a cyclic permutation of the standard scale. For example, consider the sequence E F G A B C D. Note that it also names all the notes which are white keys on the keyboard. It gives the sequence of intervals $\frac{1}{2}, 1, 1, 1, \frac{1}{2}, 1, 1$, which is different from the sequence of intervals for the standard scale. Therefore this sequence beginning with E is not equivalent to the standard scale.

One sees that the sequence of intervals $1, 1, \frac{1}{2}, 1, 1, 1, \frac{1}{2}$ for the standard scale is not equal to any of its non-trivial cyclic permutations, and hence no non-trivial permutation of the standard scale is a standard scale. This underlies the fact that the seven scales obtained by cyclicly permuting the standard scale for $i = 1, \ldots, 7$ are distinct.

The term *mode* is used in music to denote the scale in which a musical composition is most naturally accommodated. Quite often the cadences of the piece will arrive at the first scale note, or *tonic,* of the composition's mode. Each of the scales derived from the standard scale by a cyclic permutation are modes that were used and named by the Ancient Greeks. These names were incorrectly identified by the Swiss music theorist Heinrich Glarean (1488-1563) in the sixteenth century, yet it was his erroneous ecclesiastical names for the modes which became accepted. They are indicated in the chart below. The left column indicates the scale when played on the keyboard's white notes; the second column is Glarean's name for the scale; the next eight columns name the scale notes when played from C to C.

C-C	Ionian	C	D	E	F	G	A	B	C
D-D	Dorian	C	D	E$^\flat$	F	G	A	B$^\flat$	C
E-E	Phrygian	C	D$^\flat$	E$^\flat$	F	G	A$^\flat$	B$^\flat$	C
F-F	Lydian	C	D	E	F$^\sharp$	G	A	B	C
G-G	Myxolydian	C	D	E	F	G	A	B$^\flat$	C
A-A	Aeolian	C	D	E$^\flat$	F	G	A$^\flat$	B$^\flat$	C
B-B	Locrian	C	D$^\flat$	E$^\flat$	F	G$^\flat$	A$^\flat$	B$^\flat$	C

Musical Modes

Note that the key signature determines a unique scale in each of the seven modes. Hence the key signature does not determine the mode: The Ionian key of C has the same signature as the Lydian key of F, for example. To determine the mode of a composition one has to make some observations about the music, as described below.

The initial scale note of the modal scale of a composition is called the *keynote.* The keynote together with the designation of mode, e.g., B$^\flat$ Dorian, G Phrygian, or F$^\sharp$ major (see the next section), is called the *key* of the piece. Thus the key is determined by the key signature and the keynote. The keynote can usually be identified by its frequent appearance as a returning point in the melody and the root of chords, almost always including the final chord (to be explained in Chapter 3), in the harmony; it is often referred to as the *tonic,* or *tonal center,* and usually serves as a "home base" for both melody and harmony.

Major and Minor Modes. By the eighteenth century only two modes were considered satisfactory: the Ionian, which is our standard scale, and the Aeolian. These became known as the major and minor modes, respectively. With this restriction of possibilities, each key signature represents two possibilities: a major mode and a minor mode. The major mode has as its tonic the first scale note of the standard, or Ionian, scale determined by the key signature and a minor mode has as its tonic the first note of the Aeolian scale determined by the key signature. The minor key which has the same key signature as a given major key is called the *relative minor key* for that major key. The tonic of the relative minor key lies a minor third below that of the corresponding major key's tonic.

For example, no sharps or flats indicates the key of C major and the key of A minor. The character of music determines which mode prevails.

Scale Numbers and Solmization. A basic and traditional use of numerology in music is the numbering of scale tones. Numbers with a circumflex, or "hat", $\hat{1}$, $\hat{2}$, $\hat{3}$, ..., will be used to denote specific notes of the diatonic major scale. Thus in the key of $A^\flat$, $A^\flat$ is the first scale tone and is therefore denoted by $\hat{1}$. $B^\flat$ is denoted by by $\hat{2}$, C by $\hat{3}$, and so on.

$\qquad \hat{1} \quad \hat{2} \quad \hat{3} \quad \hat{4} \quad \hat{5} \quad \hat{6} \quad \hat{7} \quad \hat{8}$

If we are thinking of the diatonic scale with octave equivalence, only seven numbers are needed. However larger numbers are sometimes used in contexts where octave identification is not being assumed; for example, $\hat{9}$ indicates the diatonic note lying a ninth above some specific scale tonic $\hat{1}$.

Another common practice, called *solmization,* names the scale tones by the syllables *do, re, mi, fa, sol, la, ti.*

$\qquad$ *do* $\quad$ *re* $\quad$ *mi* $\quad$ *fa* $\quad$ *sol* $\quad$ *la* $\quad$ *ti* $\quad$ *do*

The chromatic scale tones which lie a half-step above or below diatonic notes are denoted by preceding the number with $\sharp$ or $\flat$. Hence, in the key of G, $\flat\hat{6}$ denotes $E^\flat$. (Note that this can coincide with a diatonic note, e.g., $\sharp\hat{3} = \hat{4}$.) Solmization also provides names for these tones, but we will not give them here.

Exercises

1. For the following pairs of integers m, n, find the numbers q and r whose existence is asserted in the Division Algorithm:

   (a) $17, 55$

   (b) $12, -37$

   (c) $2, 2^{21} + 3$

   (d) $7, 14k + 23$, where k is some integer

2. Sketch the graphs of these functions, and indicate how each is obtained by geometric transformations (shifts and/or stretches) of simpler functions:

   (a) $f(x) = \frac{1}{3}x - 1$

(b) $f(x) = x^2 + 1$

(c) $f(x) = \cos x + x$

3. For each of the following sets and relations determine whether or not an equivalence relation has been defined. Explain why or why not.

   (a) the set of people alive now; " has the same mother as"

   (b) $\mathbb{R}$; $\leq$

   (c) $\mathbb{Z}$; for a fixed positive integer n, $\equiv$ defined by $k \equiv \ell$ iff $n \mid (k - \ell)$

   (d) the set of notes on the piano keyboard; $\sim$ defined by $N \sim N'$ if and only if the interval between N and N' is a major third

4. For the set $\{(a,b) \in \mathbb{Z}^2 \mid b \neq 0\}$ show that the relation $\sim$ defined by $(a,b) \sim (a',b')$ iff $ab' - a'b = 0$ is an equivalence relation and that the set of equivalence classes is in one-to-one correspondence with $\mathbb{Q}$.

5. Identify these notes by letter and subscript (e.g., D_3 or $A_1^\sharp$):

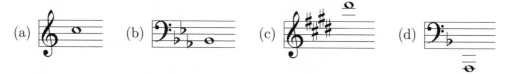

6. Identify these intervals:

7. Choosing an appropriate clef, write on staff paper, and name with subscript, the note which is:

   (a) a minor third above D_2

   (b) a fifth above $F_2^\sharp$

   (c) a major ninth below $C_6^\sharp$

   (d) a tritone below $E_4^\flat$

8. Suppose we have an eight-note scale (with first and eighth notes an octave apart) such that the sequence of intervals of adjacent notes

contains only the numbers $\frac{1}{2}$ and 1. Is it possible that this scale is a non-trivial cyclic permutation of itself? If so, give an example. If not, explain why not.

9. Answer the same question as in the last problem, but for a nine-note scale having the same property.

10. For the following modes and tonic notes, indicate the appropriate key signature on staff paper:

   (a) Lydian with tonic G

   (b) Dorian with tonic B$^\flat$

   (c) Locrian with tonic D$^\sharp$

   (d) Phrygian with tonic A

11. Transpose this melodic excerpt, written in C minor, up to E minor. Preserve the scale-tone spelling of each melody note.

Chapter 2

Horizontal Structure

In mathematics, time is often parameterized by a horizontal axis (x-axis, or t-axis). Since music is perceived through an interval of time, it is represented visually by its placement along a horizontal axis. On a musical staff the progression from left to right represents the passing of time, while the vertical axis (y-axis) designates pitch. Thus we refer to its temporal aspects, e.g., the durations of sustained notes and the sequence of events and episodes, as its *horizontal structure.* One way in which most music strives to interest and please the listener is through the presentation of temporal patterns which are satisfying and cohesive. The notation and organization of music's horizontal structure contain a number of relationships with basic mathematical concepts.

Duration of Notes. Time durations in music are often measured in *beats,* which are the temporal units by which music is notated. Frequently one beat represents the time interval by which one would "count off" the passing of time while the music is performed. The term *tempo* refers to the frequency of this count-off, usually measured in beats per minute.[1] In a musical score the basic designator of duration is, of course, the *note,* and the duration of notes is determined by such things as note heads, stem flags, dots, ties, and tuplet designations.

The durational names of notes in Western music are based on the *whole note,* which has a duration in beats (often four) dictated by the *time signature,* which will be discussed later in this chapter. Notes whose duration has proportion $1/2^n$, n a non-negative integer, with that of the whole note are

---

[1] It should be said that music is not always performed with a constant tempo; a composition may have internal tempo changes or passages performed *ad lib* or with *rubato,* in which strict tempo gives way to artistic liberty.

named according to that proportion. Thus, if the whole note has a certain duration in beats, then the *half note* has half that duration, the *quarter note* has one fourth that duration, etc. In the situation where a whole note gets four beats, then a half note gets two beats and the sixty-fourth note represents one sixteenth of a beat.

We will use the (non-standard) term *durational note* to mean a note distinguished by its <u>duration</u>, such as half note or quarter note, independent of its associated pitch. Observe that these designations for notes tacitly employ the concept of equivalence class. Here we are declaring two notes to be equivalent if they have the same duration, so that "durational note" refers to the equivalence class of all notes having a given duration (e.g., "half note" designated to the equivalence class of all half notes, regardless of their pitch). This is to be distinguished from octave equivalence, discussed in Chapter 1, whose equivalence classes are called "note classes".

The pitch of a note is dictated by the vertical position of its notehead on the staff. The duration of the note is dictated by several details which we will discuss individually. They are:

1. whether the interior of the notehead is filled

2. the presence or absence of a note stem, and, if present, the number of flags on the stem or the number of beams attached to the stem

3. the number of dots following the note, if any

4. the tuplet designation of the note, if any

Noteheads, Stems, Flags, and Beams. The whole note and half note are written with an unfilled notehead. For $n \geq 2$ the $\frac{1}{2^n}$-th note is written with a filled notehead. All $\frac{1}{2^n}$-th notes except the whole note (i.e., the case $n = 0$) possess a note stem, which either extends upward from the right side of the notehead or downward from the left side of the notehead. For $n \geq 3$, the $\frac{1}{2^n}$-th note's stem is given $n - 2$ flags. Thus an eighth note $(n = 3)$ has one flag, a sixteenth note $(n = 4)$ has two flags, etc.

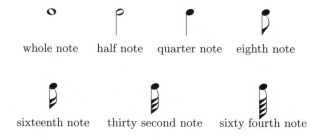

whole note   half note   quarter note   eighth note

sixteenth note   thirty second note   sixty fourth note

In adjacent notes, flags may be replaced by beams connecting the stems:

(The third example above will be clarified by the section on dots below.) Pitches which are to be sounded simultaneously may be notated by having two or more noteheads sharing a common stem, as in this passage:

Rests. A *rest* is a notational symbol which indicates silence for a duration determined by the type of rest which appears. Rests come in the same durational types as notes, distinguished by their appearance. The *whole rest,* for example, is a rectangle attached on the underside of a staff line. This and other rests are as indicated below.

| whole rest | half rest | quarter rest | eighth rest | 16th rest | 32nd rest | 64th rest |

The vertical position of rests on a staff is generally as indicated above, but not always. Some circumstances make it more desirable to place them on a higher or lower line, for example when two vocal parts (e.g., soprano and alto) share the same staff and the rest occurs in only one of the parts.

Dots. The dot beside a note or rest extends its duration by one half its original duration or, equivalently, multiplies the original duration by 3/2. Hence a dotted sixteenth note's duration in beats (still assuming for the moment that the whole note gets four beats) is given by $\frac{1}{4}(1+\frac{1}{2}) = \frac{1}{4} \cdot \frac{3}{2} = \frac{3}{8}$. A second dot beside the note calls for an additional duration of one fourth the original duration (in addition to the extra duration elicited by the first dot), so that, in the above situation, a sixteenth note with two dots has duration $\frac{1}{4}(1 + \frac{1}{2} + \frac{1}{4}) = \frac{1}{4} \cdot \frac{7}{4} = \frac{7}{16}$. Although it may seem like a purely academic exercise (since only rarely are more than two dots used), we observe that a note of duration d followed by m dots has duration d_m given by

$$d_m = d\left(1 + \frac{1}{2} + \frac{1}{2^2} + \cdots + \frac{1}{2^m}\right)$$

$$= d\sum_{i=0}^{m}\left(\frac{1}{2}\right)^i$$

$$= d\left[\frac{1 - \left(\frac{1}{2}\right)^{m+1}}{1 - \frac{1}{2}}\right] = d\left[2\left(1 - \left(\frac{1}{2}\right)^{m+1}\right)\right]$$

$$= d\left[2 - \left(\frac{1}{2}\right)^m\right] = d\left[1 + 1 - \frac{1}{2^m}\right] = d\left[1 + \frac{2^m - 1}{2^m}\right].$$

The third line in the sequence of equalities above uses the fact

$$\sum_{i=0}^{m} r^i = 1 + r + r^2 + \cdots + r^m = \frac{1 - r^{m+1}}{1 - r},$$

which holds for any integer $m \geq 0$ and any real number $r \neq 1$. The proof of this will appear as an exercise.

Perhaps the most enlightening expression for d_m in the above string of equalities is the third to last expression $d[2 - (\frac{1}{2})^m]$, which we restate:

$$\boxed{\begin{array}{c} \textit{A note of duration d followed by m dots has duration} \\ d_m = d\left[2 - \left(\frac{1}{2}\right)^m\right] \end{array}} \qquad (2.1)$$

It becomes apparent from this formula that the duration of an m-dotted note approaches $2d$ as m becomes large (d being the duration of the undotted note). This is expressed by saying $[2 - (\frac{1}{2})^m]$ approaches 2 as m tends to infinity, or

$$\lim_{m \to \infty}\left[2 - \left(\frac{1}{2}\right)^m\right] = 2.$$

It is also apparent that the value of d_m is always smaller than $2d$. The fact that the sums $\sum_{i=0}^{m}(\frac{1}{2})^i$ approach 2 as m gets large is expressed in the infinite summation

$$\sum_{i=0}^{\infty}\left(\frac{1}{2}\right)^i = 2. \qquad (2.2)$$

These notions, which involve the concept of *limit*, are made precise in calculus.

Let us use the the boxed formula (2.1) above to calculate a certain duration. Suppose we are in a context where a whole note has 2 beats (e.g., when the time signature is $\frac{2}{2}$, which will be explained later in this chapter). We then ask: What is the duration of a triply dotted sixteenth note? We first calculate the duration d of the undotted sixteenth note as $\frac{1}{16}$-th of the duration of a whole note, or $d = \frac{1}{16} \cdot 2 = \frac{1}{8}$. Here the number of dots is $m = 3$, so the formula gives

$$d_3 = \frac{1}{8}\left[2 - \left(\frac{1}{2}\right)^3\right] = \frac{1}{8}\left(2 - \frac{1}{8}\right) = \frac{1}{8} \cdot \frac{15}{8} = \frac{15}{64}.$$

The duration is $\frac{15}{64}$-ths of a beat.

Tuplets. Note that music's temporal notation is highly oriented around the prime number 2 and its powers. We do not use terms like "fifth note" or "ninth note". To divide the $\frac{1}{2^n}$-th note into k equal notes, where k is not a power of 2, we form a *k-tuplet* as follows. Find the unique positive integer r such that

$$2^r < k < 2^{r+1}$$

and notate the tuplet as a group of k $\frac{1}{2^{n+r}}$-th notes overset or underset by the integer k. The resulting tuplet is called the $\frac{1}{2^{n+r}}$-*th note k-tuplet*. This is the most basic form of *polyrhythm,* which is the imposition of simultaneous differing rhythms.

For example, suppose we wish to divide the quarter note ($\frac{1}{2^2}$-th note) into 3 equal pieces, forming a triplet. Here $n = 2$, and since $2^1 < 3 < 2^2$, we have $r = 1$. We write a sequence of 3 $\frac{1}{2^{2+1}}$-th notes, or eighth notes, overset by 3, forming an eighth note triplet. If, instead, we want to divide the quarter note into 5 notes of equal duration, we note that $2^2 < 5 < 2^3$, so $r = 2$, so we write a sequence of 5 $\frac{1}{2^{2+2}}$-th notes, or sixteenth notes, overset by 5. We call this a sixteenth note 5-tuplet.

eighth note triplet   sixteenth note 5-tuplet

The concept of dividing a unit of duration into n equal parts by an n-tuplet has an interesting similarity to the notion of the nth harmonic, which is a vibration n times faster than the vibration of a fundamental pitch. Harmonics will be discussed in Chapter 10.

Ties and Slurs. Two notes of the same pitch may be connected by a *tie,* which is a curved line that indicates they are to be considered as one note whose value is the sum of the durations of the two tied notes. Hence, if a whole note gets four beats, then the tying of a quarter note, whose duration is 1, to a dotted sixteenth, whose duration is $\frac{1}{4}(1 + \frac{1}{2}) = \frac{3}{8}$,

gives a duration of $1 + \frac{3}{8} = \frac{11}{8}$ beats.

Closely related is the *slur,* which looks like a tie but connects notes of different pitches.

This indicates to the performer that he/she should proceed from one pitch to the next with no (or minimal) rearticulation. For example, a violinist interprets this to mean the notes should be played with one stroke of the bow.

Meter. A piece of music is commonly divided into groups of n beats, for some integer $n \geq 1$. Such groups are called *measures* or *bars.* The *meter* of the piece is the number n of beats per measure together with an assignment of which durational note gets one beat's duration. These parameters are specified by the *time signature* of the piece, which is placed just after the clef symbol (and at subsequent positions if the meter changes). The time signature is comprised of two integers $\frac{n}{r}$ where $n \in \mathbb{Z}^+$ and r is a power of 2. (We refrain from writing $\frac{n}{r}$ to avoid confusion with fractions.) The meanings of n and r are given as follows:

USUAL MEANING. The top integer n specifies the number of beats to a measure and the bottom integer $r = 2^m$ designates that the $\frac{1}{2^m}$-th note gets one beat. Thus the time signature $\frac{2}{4}$ indicates 2 beats to a measure with a quarter note getting one beat.

EXCEPTIONAL CASE. 3 *divides* n <u>*and*</u> $n > 3$: In this situation we usually interpret the meter to be a *compound time signature,* which means the number of beats to a measure is taken to be $n/3$ rather than n; thus three $\frac{1}{2^m}$-th notes give one beat (where, again, $r = 2^m$). This means that one beat is signified by a dotted $\frac{1}{2^{m-1}}$-th note. Thus in $\frac{6}{8}$ time there are $6/3 = 2$ beats per measure and one beat is signified by three eighth notes, or a dotted quarter note.

In practice, the integer r in a time signature $\frac{n}{r}$ is nearly always 2, 4, or 8.

Rhythm. *Rhythm* is the way in which time is organized within measures. Consider these examples:

Upon playing these in tempo (by simply tapping) one observes that a certain amount of musical satisfaction arises from the artistic variation in the ways the measures are filled with durational notes. Rhythms can be straightforward or subtle. Jazz often avoids the obvious by temporarily obscuring the meter using complex sequences.

Sometimes certain types of rhythms are implied but not written, *swing rhythm* being the prime example. In a piece where the figure consisting of an eighth note triple with the first two notes tied is pervasive, the triplet notation becomes cumbersome and is often suppressed. The figure is simply denoted by two eighth notes. This is usually indicated by the words "swing rhythm", or a marking such as

placed above the first measure of the piece. Of course, this rhythm can be notated precisely by using one of the compound time signatures $\frac{3n}{8}$ and writing it as a quarter note followed by an eighth note.

Rules about Accidentals. It is important to know that when an accidental occurs it applies thereafter within the measure to all notes having the same note class as the altered note, unless the accidental is cancelled or changed by another accidental. When an altered note is tied to another note, the alteration on the first note applies also to the second note even if the second note lies in the next measure. In the latter situation the accidental does not apply to all notes of the same note class in the measure containing the second note. Thus, in the following excerpt all Ds are D-naturals, and the second accidental is required to effect this.

Sometimes, for the benefit of the reader, music includes accidentals which are not required according to the rules given above. Such redundant accidentals are called *cautionary accidentals,* and are enclosed in parentheses.

Melody. Melody is the succession of notes (single pitches with prescribed duration) which are most prominent in a musical composition and which serve to define and characterize the piece. Melody is the sequence of notes in a popular song that a solo vocalist sings, while other notes are being played in accompaniment. In a symphony the melody is often (but not always) played by the highest instrument, typically the first violin section.

It should be emphasized that a melody is defined and made recognizable not only by its sequence of pitches, but by its rhythm. This is exemplified by the descending scale in the Ionian (major) mode,

which by itself evokes no particular song. However, the same sequence of pitches set to the rhythm

is immediately recognized as *Joy To The World.*

Repeating Patterns. One way music achieves cohesion is through the repetition of certain melodic patterns, often with variation and embellishment. This can mean repeating a major section of the piece or, more "locally", by juxtaposing brief melodic figures. The former phenomenon will be discussed later under *form.* For the moment, however, we will discuss the local types of repetitions which correspond to the mathematical concept of geometric transformation.

Translations. A simple example of such is a horizontal shift, or *translation,* which is effected in the graph of a function $y = f(x)$ when we replace it by $y = f(x - c)$ (see Chapter 1). This often appears in music as the repetitions (horizontal translation) of the sequence of pitches or the rhythmic pattern. Here is a familiar example which illustrates rhythmic translation:

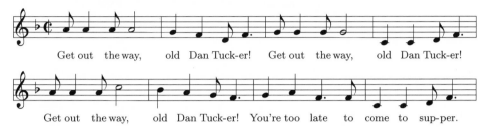

Note that the rhythm of the first two bars is repeated twice, while the sequence of pitches varies.

An example of melodic (as well as rhythmic) translation is found in the spiritual *When The Saints Go Marching In,*[2]

where the melodic sequence F-A-B♭-C appears three times consecutively.

Transposition. When a repeating pattern is being represented melodically, it is possible to also apply a vertical shift or *transposition,* analogous to replacing the graph of $y = f(x)$ by that of $y = f(x) + c$. Such a shift may repeat a melodic excerpt, transposing each note upward or downward by a fixed chromatic interval, as in the first sixteen bars of George and Ira Gershwin's *Strike Up The Band,* in which the second eight measures repeat the melody of the first, transposed up by the interval of a fourth.

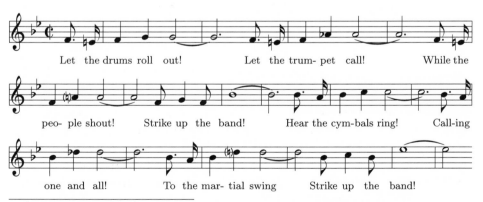

---

[2]This example is given in [4], as are the excerpts from *O Tannenbaum* and *Raindrops Keep Falling On My Head,* which appear a little later in this discussion.

This type of transposition exemplified above is called *chromatic transposition.*

A variant form of transposition, called *diatonic transposition,* occurs when a diatonic melody is moved up or down by the same number of diatonic scale tones, producing a melody having the same general shape, but with chromatic intervals not perfectly preserved due to the differing intervals between adjacent diatonic notes. This occurs on the German Carol *O Tannenbaum (O Christmas Tree).* Note that the first bracketed sequence below is shifted downward by one diatonic scale tone in the second bracketed sequence.

Retrogression. Yet another form of transformation in music is *retrogression,* which is analogous to the mathematical notion of horizontal reflection. Such a reflection is exemplified when we replace the graph of $y = f(x)$ with that of $y = -f(x)$, reflecting the graph around the y-axis. In music, "retrogression" means "inverting the order of notes", so that the resulting sequence forms a reflection of the initial one. In this excerpt from *Raindrops Keep Falling On My Head,* note the symmetry of the melody around the point designated by $\wedge$:

Form. The sequence of larger sections of music into which music may be organized is sometimes called *form.* The number of measures in a section is often a power of 2. For example, ragtime compositions typically consist of three or four sections, each section having 16 measures; sometimes one or more of these sections is repeated once. These sections are distinguishable by the listener by virtue of different rhythmic and melodic character. If a composition consisted of three sections, we might denote the form by: ABC. If the first two sections were repeated, the form would be AA BB C. Scott

Joplin's (1868-1917) *Maple Leaf Rag* has the form AA BB A CC DD.

Two classical type forms are *binary form* and *ternary form.* The former presents a piece of music as two main sections which are repeated, giving a form AABB. Many of the minuets and scherzos of the late 18th and 19th centuries have this form. Ternary form presents three sections, with the first and third being the same, or very similar, giving C pattern ABA. It often is found in the nocturnes of Frédérik Chopin (1810-1849) and the piano pieces of Johannes Brahms (1833-1897).

Most songs in American popular music and folk music can be naturally divided into 8-bar segments, some of which typically recur. One common pattern is AABA, exemplified by the Tin Pan Alley song *Five Foot Two, Eyes of Blue.* If a section bears strong resemblance to another, it may be given the same letter followed by '. For example, the form of the song *Edelweiss* is represented by AA'BA'.

Symmetry. The word *symmetry* is used in music in general reference to the phenomena of transformations and repeating sections. A compositional goal in many styles of music is to create balanced portions of unity and contrast - enough repetition to give a piece interest and cohesion, but not so much as to make it repetitive or boring. As an example of a simple piece which illustrates the use of multiple symmetries, let us refer back to the carol *O Tannenbaum.* Here the form of the complete chorus is AABA, but each section has internal symmetries as well. Both the A and B sections incorporate melodic transposition and rhythmic translation, with the B section featuring a downward diatonic transposition, discussed earlier in this chapter.

Exercises

1. In $\frac{4}{4}$ time, give the duration in beats for:

   (a) a dotted thirty-second note

   (b) a half note with four dots

   (c) a quarter note tied to a sixteenth note with three dots

2. In $\frac{12}{8}$ time, taken as a compound time signature, give the duration in beats for:

   (a) a dotted eighth note

   (b) a quarter note tied to a sixteenth note

   (c) a thirty-second note with three dots

3. Prove the equation:

$$1 + r + r^2 + \cdots + r^m = \frac{1 - r^{m+1}}{1 - r}$$

for any integer $m \geq 0$ and any real number $r \neq 1$. (Hint: Consider the product $(1 - r)(1 + r + r^2 + \cdots + r^m)$.)

4. Notate and name the following tuplets:

(a) that which divides the quarter note into 5 equal notes

(b) that which divides the eighth note into 3 equal notes

(c) that which divides the whole note into 11 equal notes

5. Notate and give the total duration, in $\frac{4}{4}$ time, of:

(a) a sixteenth note septuplet

(b) a half note triplet

(c) a quarter note 17-tuplet

6. Complete these measures with a single durational note:

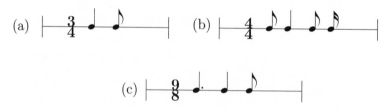

7. Complete the following excerpt three ways with a measure having the same rhythm,

employing, respectively:

(a) diatonic transposition up one scale tone

(b) diatonic transposition up three scale tones

(c) chromatic transposition up a minor third

Which of these, if any, represents <u>both</u> diatonic and chromatic transposition?

8. Which fractions of a whole note can be achieved using only $\frac{1}{2^n}$-notes, for various n, along with dots and ties? Justify your answer.

9. Give the form (e.g., ABAC or ABA) of the following songs (one chorus only):

   (a) *Let Me Call You Sweetheart*

   (b) *My Bonnie Lies Over The Ocean*

   (c) *Let It Be*

   (d) *The Rose*

10. For the <u>refrain</u> of the song *Someone To Watch Over Me,* by George Gershwin and Ira Gershwin, give the form (e.g., ABAC or ABA) by dividing the refrain into segments consisting of eight measures.

    For the same refrain, locate transformations such as translation (melodic and/or rhythmic) and transposition (diatonic and/or chromatic), other than those that are dictated by the global form determined above.

Chapter 3

Harmony and Related Numerology

Harmony. *Harmony* is that aspect of music in which different pitches are sounded simultaneously. The earliest harmony in Western music consisted of parallel octaves, fourths and fifths. Over the centuries a rich array of harmonic patterns and clichès has evolved, and later we will examine some of these patterns and the role mathematics played in their development. The basic harmonic building block is the *chord,* which is a collection of notes, usually three or more, sounded simultaneously. Chords have a type which is determined by the intervals, modulo octave, between the notes in the chord. A chord also has a numerical label which is determined by its juxtaposition with the tonic note of the key.

Intervals and Modular Arithmetic. Before launching our discussion of harmony, we introduce the notion of modular integers, which allows us to refine the notion of modular interval as defined in Chapter 1.

It was given in an exercise in Chapter 1 to show that, for a fixed integer $n \in \mathbb{Z}^+$, the relation $k \equiv \ell$ defined by $n \mid (k - \ell)$ is an equivalence relation on the set of integers $\mathbb{Z}$. We express this relationship by saying "k is congruent to ℓ modulo n", or $k \equiv \ell \mod n$. It is easily seen that $k \equiv \ell \mod n$ if and only if k and ℓ have the same remainder r obtained from n using the Division Algorithm: $k = qn + r$ (see Chapter 1), and that each equivalence class contains precisely one of the integers $\{0, 1, 2, \ldots, n - 1\}$. Hence there are m equivalence classes. We denote the set of equivalence classes by $\mathbb{Z}_n$.

The case $n = 12$ has a special significance in music, as follows. By measuring intervals in semitones, the set of intervals is identified with the set $\mathbb{Z}$

of integers, with an integer k corresponding to the interval of k semitones, upward if k is positive, downward if k is negative. With this identification, equivalence modulo 12 is nothing more than octave identification: Two intervals measured in semitones by integers k and ℓ are equivalent modulo octave if and only if $k \equiv \ell \mod 12$. Accordingly, each equivalence class of intervals contains a unique interval of r semitones with $0 \le r < 12$ (i.e., a non-negative interval less than an octave), and this r is obtained as the remainder in the Division Algorithm with $n = 12$.

For example, the interval of a ninth, which is 14 semitones, is equivalent to the interval of a step, 2 semitones, since $14 \equiv 2 \mod 12$. Similarly, one verifies that down a fourth is equivalent to up a fifth, since $-5 \equiv 7 \mod 12$.

In some contexts when we speak of musical intervals, we actually mean interval classes modulo octave, of which there are twelve. We will try to make this distinction clear at all times. Note that there is a well-defined interval class between any ordered pair of note classes, which can be represented uniquely by a non-negative interval less than an octave. For example, the interval from $\mathrm{E}^\flat$ to B is represented by 8 semitones, or a minor sixth.

Major Chord. The first chord we will consider is the *major* chord, which consists of a note sounded simultaneously with the notes which lie a major third and a fifth above the given note. Below are some examples of major chords:

The note of the major chord which has chord notes lying a major third and a fifth above it is called the *root*. The two subsequent notes are called the *third* and *fifth*, respectively. Thus in the middle example above, the root of the major chord is F, the third is A, and the fifth is C.

In general, chords are defined by the <u>note classes</u> (and modular intervals) they employ. Thus any of the notes in a chord may be displaced and/or doubled by the interval of one or more octaves. Hence the following variations are also major chords.

Voicing. The term *voicing* is used to denote the particular way a chord is written, i.e., the specific notes, as opposed to note classes, which are chosen. Observe that the root need not be the bottom note. In the rightmost voicing above, the lowest note is the fifth of the major chord. But observe that, regardless of the voicing, there is no ambiguity about which note is the root, third, or fifth of a major chord. That is because, like the standard scale, the sequence of modular intervals $(4, 3, 5)$ (measured in semitones by elements of $\mathbb{Z}_{12}$) between successive note classes comprising the major chord

$$\text{root} \xrightarrow{4} \text{third} \xrightarrow{3} \text{fifth} \xrightarrow{5} (\text{root})$$

has the property that no non-trivial cyclic permutation of the sequence gives the same sequence, in other words it has no *non-trivial cyclic symmetries*.

Minor Chord. The *minor* chord is defined by the sequence of modular intervals $(3, 4, 5)$. Thus it consists of a root together with the notes which lie a minor third and a fifth, modulo octave, above the root. As with the major chord, the two successive tones are called third and fifth,

$$\text{root} \xrightarrow{3} \text{third} \xrightarrow{4} \text{fifth} \xrightarrow{5} (\text{root})$$

and again the root, third, and fifth are uniquely determined by the sequence of modular intervals. Here are some minor chords.

Triads. Chords which contain exactly three notes, modulo octave, are called *triads*. The major and minor chords are examples. Triads have been a fundamental part of harmony in Western music since the seventeenth century. The term *triadic* is sometimes applied to music that primarily features triads.

To avoid any possible confusion between the major chord and other chords that contain the major chord (to be introduced below), we often refer to the major chord as the *major triad*. Similarly we use the term *minor triad* for the minor chord.

Diminished and Augmented Chords. Two other triads which play significant roles in Western music are the *diminished* chord, defined by the sequence of modular intervals $(3, 3, 6)$, and the *augmented* chord, defined by the sequence $(4, 4, 4)$.

diminished   augmented

Note that the augmented chord, unlike all the previously introduced chords, has no discernable root. Any cyclic permutation of its sequence of intervals gives the same sequence.

Seventh Chord. We now introduce some important four-note chords. The first is the *seventh* chord, defined by the sequence of intervals $(4, 3, 3, 2)$. The notes are called root, third, fifth, and seventh, respectively.

$$\text{root} \xrightarrow{\ 4\ } \text{third} \xrightarrow{\ 3\ } \text{fifth} \xrightarrow{\ 3\ } \text{seventh} \ (\xrightarrow{\ 2\ } \text{root})$$

This sequence has no non-trivial cyclic symmetries, hence the root, third, fifth, and seventh are distinguishable. Examples are:

Observe that this chord contains the major chord with the same root, third, and fifth. We will later say quite a bit about this chord's role in the development of Western harmony and the tuning obstacles associated with it.

Minor Seventh Chord. Another four-note chord to be introduced here is the *minor seventh,* defined by the sequence $(3, 4, 3, 2)$, which admits no non-trivial cyclic symmetries. Its notes are also called root, third, fifth, and seventh. Here are examples.

The minor seventh chord contains the minor chord having the same root, third, and fifth.

Major Seventh Chord. A somewhat dissonant variation is the *major seventh* chord, which has the sequence $(4, 3, 4, 1)$. It also admits no non-trivial cyclic symmetries. Observe that it, like the seventh chord, contains the major triad, the difference being that the interval from the fifth to the seventh is a major third rather than a minor third.

This type of harmony became popular in the twentieth century, and is one of the characteristic sounds of "smooth jazz". The dissonance arises with the semitone interval between the note class of the seventh and that of the root.

Diminished Seventh. The *diminished seventh,* or *full diminished,* chord is defined by the sequence of modular intervals $(3, 3, 3, 3)$. Like the augmented chord, every cyclic permutation of its sequence gives the same sequence, so it too has no discernable root. Here are two examples:

This chord imparts a feeling of tension or instability. It often resolves to a more consonant chord, such as a major or minor triad.

Half-Diminished Seventh. The *half-diminished seventh* chord is defined by the sequence of modular intervals $(3, 3, 4, 2)$. It has a discernable root, having no non-trivial cyclic permutations. Examples:

This chord also has a somewhat unstable aura and suggests the need for resolution. Like the seventh, it often resolves around the circle of fifths.

Chord Labeling. Chords are often labeled and/or denoted by identifying the root followed by a suffix which indicates the type of chord. The root can be labeled by identifying a specific note class, such as D or B$^\flat$, or a scale tone. In the latter case the scale tone is indicated by a Roman numeral, possibly preceded by $\sharp$ or $\flat$, such as III or $\flat$VI. For this the proper mode must be incorporated.

There are various conventions for writing the suffix which indicates the chord type. We will adhere to the following notations for these suffixes:

- major triad: no suffix

- minor triad: m

- augmented: aug or $^{+}$

- diminished: dim or ^{0}

- seventh: ^{7}

- minor seventh: m^{7}

- major seventh: M^{7}

- diminished seventh: ^{07}

- half-diminished seventh: $^{\emptyset 7}$

For example, a major triad whose root is C is denoted by C. In the key of F major, it would be denoted V. In the key of A minor, it would be denoted III. The minor seventh chord whose root is F$^\sharp$ is denoted F$^\sharp$m^{7}. In the key of D major, it would be IIIm^{7}. In the key of G minor, it would be denoted $\sharp$VIIm^{7}. We often label augmented or diminished seventh chords, which have no discernable root, by declaring the root to be the lowest note in its voicing.

Here are some chords labeled according to the note class of the root.

Below are some chords labeled according to the scale tone numeral of the root. Here we assume the major (Ionian) mode.

Chapter 11 will present mathematical reasons why certain chords seem to possess a "harmonious", or consonant, quality, while others have a more "clashing", or dissonant, effect.

Alternate Chord Labeling. Another quite common method of chord labeling uses uppercase and lowercase letters/numerals to indicate whether the third of the chord is major or minor, respectively. Thus a minor seventh chord rooted on $B^\flat$ would be denoted $b^{\flat 7}$ and a minor triad rooted on scale tone $\hat{4}$ is written iv. All other suffixes are the same, generally choosing the second alternatives listed above for the diminished and augmented triads. Thus the diminished triad on $\hat{2}$ is written ii^0.

Chord Spelling. As we noted in Chapter 1, the use of accidentals enables any keyboard note to be written more than one way. For example, $A^\sharp$ renders the same pitch as $B^\flat$, and G is $A^{\flat\flat}$. In musical notation, the term "spelling" refers to the choice of this representation for a given note, or for the notes in a given chord. Musicians generally prefer that written music adheres to certain rules in the spelling of chords.

In order to explain the correct spelling of chords, we will for the moment adopt the term *spelled notes* to refer to a note or note class as notated. Spelled notes, then, differentiate between different notes spellings which are enharmonically the same; thus $A^\sharp$ is a different spelled note class from $B^\flat$. Also, for any spelled note (class) we define its *underlying unaltered note (class)* to be the class obtained by stripping away accidentals from the note, in the ambient key. Thus, in the key of C major, A is the underlying unaltered note class of A♯; in the key of B minor, C♯ is the underlying unaltered note class of C♮. Obviously the underlying unaltered note, or note class, always lies on a diatonic scale tone.

Correct spelling can now be explained in the following way. The third of a chord should be spelled so that its underlying unaltered note class is two scale tone classes above that of the root; the fifth of a chord should be spelled so that its underlying unaltered note class is four scale tone classes above that of the root; and the seventh of a chord should be spelled so that its underlying unaltered note class is six scale tone classes above that of the root.

As an example, if the root of a major chord is spelled as C♯, then its third should be spelled as E♯, not F. Below are two examples of misspelled chords followed by the same enharmonic chord with correct spelling. Note that in the first example (D) the third is misspelled and in the second example (E♭7) both fifth and seventh are misspelled.

D misspelled   D   E♭7 misspelled   E♭7

Correct spelling often necessitates the use of double flats, double sharps, and non-diatonic notes which have diatonic enharmonic equivalents. Consider these examples:

♯II7 in B major   ♭III in A♭ major

For augmented and diminished seventh chords, whose roots cannot be determined merely from the chords' pitch classes, correct spelling will identify the root. Rules of spelling, however, tend to be followed less rigorously for these chords, as well as for diminished triads. Note, for example, that the I dim chord in the example is misspelled. The first example below gives the correct spelling of C07. The middle chord of the second example gives the same enharmonic chord spelled as D♯07; however in some contexts (such as the one that appears here) this chord might be viewed as a misspelling of $C^{\varnothing 7}$.

C⁰⁷   C⁷   ?   C⁷

In the following example the middle chord, because of context, would likely be labeled as E aug, even though it is spelled as C aug (here the sharp applies throughout, since there is no bar line) to allow the augmented fifth to be written diatonically as C rather than B♯.

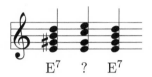

E⁷   ?   E⁷

In some cases music gives a different name to an alternate spelling of a chord. We will not delve much into this, but an example that comes to mind is the augmented sixth chord, which is enharmonically equivalent to the seventh chord but spells the seventh as an augmented sixth, as in the first chord of the example below.

We will not discuss the matter of when and why the chord might be written as an augmented sixth rather than seventh chord except to say that if it appears in a "dominant" role, that is, when it leads around the circle of fifths (see below), it should always be spelled as a seventh chord.

Finally, it should be admitted that chords are sometimes intentionally misspelled simply to make the voice leading more natural and/or readable to the vocalist or instrumentalist.

Progressions. Musical "character" is created in part by the way various chord types are organized and juxtaposed in real time. The procedure from one chord to the next is called *progression.* A certain amount of musical satisfaction is obtained merely from a pleasing or catchy sequence of progressions. Certain patterns are common, thus giving musical clichés that are quite familiar to most listeners.

A classical example is a progression in which the root moves counter-clockwise around the circle of fifths, depicted below.

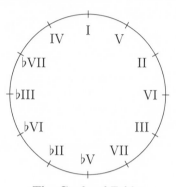

The Circle of Fifths

Note that as we proceed clockwise the progressions go up a fifth, or, equivalently modulo octave, down a fourth; as we proceed counter-clockwise the progressions are up a fourth, or down a fifth. (Note also that each chromatic scale tone occupies one and only one clock position. We say more about this later.) The classical circle-of-fifths progression is one in which the root of a chord is a fourth above the root of the preceding chord. In other words the root movement goes counter-clockwise, as in the sequence of major mode progressions:

$$VI^7 \longrightarrow II\,m \longrightarrow V^7 \longrightarrow I$$

Often a melody suggests the chords which should underlie it by offering a sequence of notes which lie mostly within a certain chord. Sometimes this basic "implied harmony" can be artistically altered or enhanced. For example, this melody, in F major,

is comfortably accommodated by the sequence $I \to V^7 \to I$ (or $F \to C^7 \to F$), each chord sustained or played in arpeggio for one measure. All the melody notes lie within the respective chords except for the D in the second measure, which doesn't lie in C^7. But observe that the following harmonizations also work,

$$I \longrightarrow II\,m \longrightarrow III\,m$$

$$\text{I} \longrightarrow \text{IV} \longrightarrow \text{V}$$

$$\text{I} \longrightarrow \flat\text{VII} \longrightarrow \text{I}$$

$$\text{I} \longrightarrow \flat\text{VII} \longrightarrow \text{V}$$

each giving the passage a different personality.

Exercises

1. Identify these chords by root note and suffix (e.g., $B\,m^7$ or $E^\flat\,aug$):

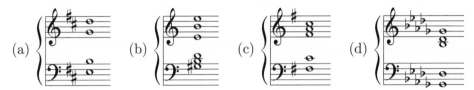

2. Identify these chords by root scale tone and suffix (e.g., V^7 or $\sharp\text{II}\,m$). Assume the major mode in (a) and (b), the minor mode in (c), and the Dorian mode in (d).

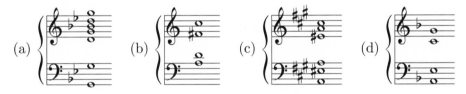

3. Write these chords with correct spelling on the treble clef:

(a) Dm^7 (b) $E^\flat dim$ (c) $A^{\flat\emptyset7}$ (d) $F^{\sharp7}$ (e) GM^7

4. Write these chords with correct spelling on the bass clef:

(a) $E^\flat m^7$ (b) $D\,dim$ (c) $G^\flat$ (d) $C^{\sharp7}$ (e) $B^\flat\,aug$

5. Write these chords with correct spelling, across the bass and treble clefs, in the indicated (major) key signature:

(a) II^7 in the key of D major

(b) IVm^7 in the key of $A^\flat major$

(c) I aug in the key of F major

(d) $V^{\emptyset 7}$ in the key of B major

(e) ♭VII in the Lydian key of $E^\flat$

6. Name the chord given by each of these sequences of semitones:

   (a) 4,5   (b) 2,4,3   (c) 6,3,6   (d) 7,8,7   (e) 16,6,9,5,7

   Name the chord given by each of these sequences of intervals:

   (a) fifth, fourth, major third, tritone

   (b) major third, minor sixth, major sixth

   (c) fifth, octave, minor third, tritone

   (d) step, fifth, major sixth

   (e) minor third, minor third, step

7. For each of the types of chords discussed in the text, list by Roman numeral all the ways the chord can be created using only <u>diatonic</u> note classes in the major mode.

8. Consider the chord obtained by taking the seventh chord and flatting its fifth. Such a chord is sometimes labeled with the suffix $^{7-5}$. Show that this chord does not have a discernable root. Write an example of such a chord and give all possible labelings of it.

9. In a given mode, the chord consisting of scale tones $\hat{1}$, $\hat{3}$, and $\hat{5}$ is called the *tonic triad*. For each of the seven modes introduced in Chapter 1, determine the chord type of its tonic triad.

10. For each of the seven modes, classify the chord consisting of scale tones $\hat{2}$, $\hat{4}$, $\hat{6}$, and $\hat{8}$ ($=\hat{1}$).

11. Identify each chord in the following minor mode (Aeolian) passage. Above the staff label each chord by root note class with suffix (e.g., $E^{\flat 7}$). Below the staff, label each chord by root scale tone (e.g., ♭III^7). Also, one of the chords could be considered misspelled. Which chord is it?

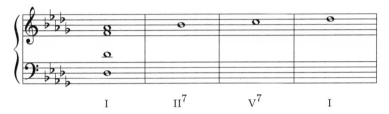

12. Complete the following to a four-part harmonization of the given melody, written in the major mode, using only whole notes, so that the melody is the top part and the bottom note is always the root. The chords should be those indicated under the staff.

13. Give a plausible harmonization of this melody by providing, in the bass clef, one whole note chord for each measure. Label each chord by root scale tone (Roman numeral) and chord type (e.g., IIm^7).

14. Analyze the basic harmony in the first 16 measures of Scott Joplin's *Maple Leaf Rag*. Each measure will have at most two chords. Label the chords by root note class and chord type (e.g., G^7). (Note: In a few places the chords are incomplete.)

15. Analyze the basic harmony in the first five measures of Ludwig van Beethoven's *Moonlight Sonata*. Label the chords by root note class and chord type (e.g., G^7).

Chapter 4

Ratios and Musical Intervals

We like to think of an interval as the "distance" between two pitches. The most basic interval is the octave. If one hears the pitches 440 Hz (A_4) and 880 Hz, one recognizes the latter as being one octave above the former, hence 880 Hz is A_5. The pitch 220 is one octave below A_4, hence is A_3. The difference between the frequencies of A_3 and A_4 is 220, while the difference between the frequencies of A_4 and A_5 is 440, yet the intervals are the same – one octave. This reflects the fact that the octave corresponds to a factor of 2, and that an interval should not be associated with the difference between the two frequencies, but rather the <u>ratio</u> between the two frequencies.

The Equivalence Relation of Ratios. Consider the relation on the set of ordered pairs from $\mathbb{R}^+$ (i.e., the set $(\mathbb{R}^+)^2$) which declares two pairs (a, b) and (a', b') to be related if the ratios of their coordinates are equal, that is, if $\frac{a}{b} = \frac{a'}{b'}$, which is equivalent to saying $a'b = ab'$. One easily verifies that this defines an equivalence relation on $(\mathbb{R}^+)^2$. Note, for example, that $(2 : 3) = (4 : 6) = (\frac{1}{2} : \frac{3}{4})$. We denote the equivalence class of $(a, b) \in (\mathbb{R}^+)^2$ by $(a : b)$, or sometimes just $a : b$, and we call it the *ratio* of a and b. Denoting the set of equivalence classes by $(\mathbb{R}^+ : \mathbb{R}^+)$, we see that the function

$$\varphi : \left(\mathbb{R}^+ : \mathbb{R}^+\right) \to \mathbb{R}^+ \text{ defined by } \varphi((a : b)) = \frac{a}{b} \tag{4.1}$$

is well defined, and that it is one-to-one and onto.

The Ratio Associated to an Interval. Since we have identified the set $\mathbb{R}^+$ with the set of pitches, or frequencies, the equivalence relation defined above applies to pairs of pitches (f_2, f_1), placing such a pair in an equivalence class $f_2 : f_1$, which is associated via φ to the number $r = \frac{f_2}{f_1}$ which we also call the ratio of f_2 to f_1. This number r is a measurement of the interval from the pitch f_1 to the pitch f_2. We will refer to both r and the corresponding class $f_2 : f_1$ as the *interval*, or *interval ratio*, determined by the frequencies f_1 and f_2. Thus each $r \in \mathbb{R}^+$ gives a unique interval. It is an enlightening exercise to listen to the intervals determined by various ratios r, such as 3, 3/2, $\sqrt{2}$, 0.7, and even the transcendental numbers $\pi \approx 3.14159$ and $e \approx 2.71828$.

Orientation of Intervals. Intervals have an upward or downward orientation. We say that the interval given by pitches (f_2, f_1) (which we read as the interval from f_1 to f_2) is *upward* if $f_2 > f_1$ and *downward* if $f_2 < f_1$. In the former case we have $\frac{f_2}{f_1} > 1$; in the latter case $\frac{f_2}{f_1} < 1$. Thus the upward intervals are given by the real numbers x which are greater than 1, and the downward intervals are given by the positive real numbers x which are less than 1:

$$\text{set of downward intervals} = \{x \in \mathbb{R} \mid 0 < x < 1\} = (0, 1),$$
$$\text{set of upward intervals} = \{x \in \mathbb{R} \mid 1 < x\} = (0, \infty).$$

The interval created when $f_1 = f_2$ will here be called the *unison interval*. It is given by the ratio $f : f$ (for any $f \in \mathbb{R}^+$), which corresponds via φ to the number 1.

Each interval $f_2 : f_1$ has a unique *opposite interval*, given by the ratio $f_1 : f_2$. It is the interval having the same "distance" in the opposite direction: if $f_2 : f_1$ is upward, then $f_1 : f_2$ is downward, and vice-versa. If r is the real number ratio of an interval, then its opposite interval has ratio r^{-1}.

If the orientation of an interval is not stated, it will be assumed that an upward interval is meant. For example if we say "the interval of a fourth", this will be taken to mean "the upward interval of a fourth".

Multiplicativity. Observe that intervals have the following multiplicative property: If x_1 represents the interval $f_2 : f_1$ and x_2 the interval $f_3 : f_2$, then $x_1 x_2$ represents the interval $f_3 : f_1$. This is obvious, since $x_1 x_2 = \frac{f_2}{f_1} \frac{f_3}{f_2} = \frac{f_3}{f_1}$. Thus the result of juxtaposing two intervals, i.e., following one interval by another, is given by multiplying the two corresponding real numbers.

Multiplicative and Additive Measurements. The measurement of intervals by ratio is called *multiplicative*, because of the property stated above. The usual measurements of intervals, such as semitones, steps, or octaves, are called *additive* because when we juxtapose two intervals we think of adding or subtracting. For example we say that 2 semitones plus 3 semitones equals 5 semitones; a fifth is a major third plus a minor third; a semitone is a major sixth minus a minor sixth. We will show later how this more conventional notion of interval relates to the multiplicative notion of an interval as a ratio.

Semitones. The principle of multiplicativity enables one to determine which real number gives the interval of a semitone. Let us denote this number by s. Since twelve iterations of this interval gives the octave, which has ratio 2, we must have $s^{12} = 2$, which says (since s is positive)

$$s = \sqrt[12]{2} = 2^{1/12}.$$

If we iterate this interval n times to get n semitones, the ratio will be $\left(2^{1/12}\right)^n = 2^{n/12}$. It is natural to extend this conversion formula to an interval measured in semitones x, for any $x \in \mathbb{R}^+$:

$$\boxed{\text{The interval of } x \text{ semitones has ratio } 2^{x/12}.} \qquad (4.2)$$

This just follows from the fact that $\left(2^{1/12}\right)^n = 2^{n/12}$.

Examples. The interval of a major third (4 semitones) has the ratio $2^{4/12} = 2^{1/3} = \sqrt[3]{2} \approx 1.25992$. The interval of downward a minor third (-3 semitones) has ratio $2^{-3/12} = 2^{-1/4} = 1/\sqrt[4]{2} \approx 0.840896$.

Frequencies of Keyboard Notes. If a note N has frequency f and an interval has ratio r, the note which lies the interval r from N has frequency rf. Given that A_4 is tuned to 440 Hz, we can now use a calculator to obtain the frequency of any other note on the keyboard.

For example, using the above calculation of the major third's ratio as $2^{1/3}$, we calculate in hertz the frequency f of $C_4^\sharp$, which lies a major third above A_3.

Since A_3 has frequency 220 Hz (being one octave below A_4) we have

$$f = 220 \cdot 2^{1/3} \approx 277.18.$$

Therefore $C_4^\sharp$ should be tuned to 277.18 Hz.

Microtuning and Cents. We will see later that mathematical tuning involves intervals which cannot be realized as integer multiples of semitones.

The term *microtuning* refers to systems of tuning which alter the frequencies of notes in the equally tempered chromatic scale, or which add new notes to that scale.

For this the semitone is divided into 100 equal intervals, the subdivision being called a *cent*. Thus 1200 iterations of this interval gives an octave. The interval of one cent is so small as to be imperceptible to most of us. Even the interval of 10 cents is difficult to perceive. Therefore the measurement of intervals in cents is fine enough to be quite satisfactory for microtuning.

Cents, like semitones and octaves, is an additive measurement of intervals.

Conversion of Cents to a Ratio. Let c denote the ratio corresponding to one cent. Then by reasoning as we did with semitones, we have $c^{1200} = 2$, i.e.,

$$c = 2^{1/1200} \approx 1.0005778 \,.$$

For any number x (not necessarily an integer), the interval of x cents has the ratio r given by

$$r = c^x = \left(2^{1/1200}\right)^x = 2^{x/1200} \,.$$

Thus $r = 2^{x/1200}$ gives the conversion of x cents to a ratio r.

$$\boxed{\text{The interval of } x \text{ cents has ratio } 2^{x/1200}.} \qquad (4.3)$$

This relationship allows us to convert cents to a ratio using a scientific calculator. For example, the interval of 17 cents corresponds to the number $2^{17/1200} \approx 1.009868$.

Arbitrary Chromatic Units. Suppose n is a positive integer and we wish to divide the octave into n equal subintervals, which we will call *n-chromatic units*. The same reasoning that led to formulas (4.2) and (4.3) tells us that:

$$\boxed{\text{The interval of } x \text{ } n\text{-chromatic units has ratio } 2^{x/n}.} \qquad (4.4)$$

Octave Equivalence of Interval Ratios. By definition, two intervals are equivalent modulo octave if they differ by an interval of n octaves, for some $n \in \mathbb{Z}$. The difference of two intervals is the result of juxtaposing the first with the opposite of the second. If the intervals are given by ratios r_1 and r_2, this difference is given by the interval ratio $r_1 r_2^{-1}$. The interval of n octaves has ratio 2^n. Thus we have:

PROPOSITION. *Two interval ratios r_1 and r_2 are equivalent modulo octave if and only if there exists $n \in \mathbb{Z}$ such that $r_1 r_2^{-1} = 2^n$.*

For example, the interval ratios 41 and 328 are equivalent modulo octave, since $\frac{41}{328} = \frac{1}{8} = 2^{-3}$.

Conversion to Additive Measurements. We eventually will need to be able to convert the ratio measurement of a musical interval to an additive measurement such as cents or semitones. Suppose we are given a ratio r to convert to cents. In this situation we must solve for x in the equation $r = 2^{x/1200}$. This requires taking a *logarithm*, a topic which will be reviewed and developed in the next section. The following observation provides additional motivation for evoking logarithms. If we plot pitches on an axis according to their frequency, we see that musical intervals are not represented as distance along the axis. For example, the pitches A_2, A_3, A_4, and A_5 appear as:

$$
\begin{array}{ccccc}
A_2 & A_3 & A_4 & & A_5 \\
\hline
0 \quad 110 & 220 & 440 & & 880
\end{array}
$$

The distances on the frequency axis between A_n, A_{n+1} for various integers n are different though the musical intervals are all the same – one octave. This is somewhat unsatisfying since we are used to thinking of two pairs of pitches representing the same interval as being the same "distance" apart, which is roughly the situation on a musical staff, where the vertical "distance" between each successive A, notated on the same clef, appears to be the same:

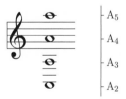

However if we plot the pitches according to the logarithms of their frequencies, we get a more satisfying result. The logarithm will also enable us to measure in semitones an interval expressed as a ratio r or given by a ratio of two frequencies $f_1 : f_2$.

Vibration of Strings. It was known by the Ancient Greeks that the vibrating frequency of a string is inversely proportional to the length of the string, provided the tension on the string and the weight of the string per unit of length remain the same. This says the relationship between length L and frequency F can be expressed as

$$F = \frac{k}{L} \tag{4.5}$$

for some $k \in \mathbb{R}^+$.

Some stringed instruments, such as guitars, have frets so that the length of the string, and hence the pitch it sounds when strummed, can be altered in performance. This is effected with a greater degree of freedom in stringed instruments which do not have a fret, such as violins, where the instrumentalist's finger holds the string tightly against the fingerboard of the instrument, thus changing the length of the vibrating portion of the string.

Let us consider how the fret (or, equivalently, the position of the instrumentalist's finger on an unfretted instrument) can be positioned to effect a given change of frequency. Suppose the string has length L and its frequency is F. Visualize the string stretching horizontally, and suppose a fret is positioned at distance L' from, say, the right end of the string.

We want to calculate the interval ratio $F' : F$, where F' is the frequency of the segment of string to the right of the fret. This segment has length L', so by (4.5) we have

$$F' : F = \left(\frac{k}{L'} : \frac{k}{L} \right) = \left(\frac{1}{L'} : \frac{1}{L} \right),$$

which corresponds, via the function φ defined in (4.1) to the number

$$\varphi(F' : F) = \frac{\frac{1}{L'}}{\frac{1}{L}} = \frac{L}{L'}.$$

If L' is expressed in terms of its proportion to L, i.e., $L' = qL$, the fraction becomes

$$\frac{L}{qL} = \frac{1}{q}.$$

Putting this together, we have

$$\frac{F'}{F} = \frac{1}{q}. \tag{4.6}$$

So suppose we want to place a fret so as to move the pitch upward by a specified ratio $r \geq 1$. This means $r = \frac{F'}{F} = \frac{1}{q}$, by (4.6), hence

$$\boxed{q = r^{-1}.} \tag{4.7}$$

Example. Suppose we want to place a fret so as to move the pitch upward a major third above F. Since the major third has ratio $r = 2^{1/3}$, we have $q = \left(2^{1/3}\right)^{-1} = 2^{-1/3} \approx 0.7937$. The position of the fret is $(0.7937)L$, which is close to $(0.8)L = \frac{4}{5}L$.

Exercises

1. Express each of the following intervals as elements of $\mathbb{R}^+$ three ways: (1) as a radical or the reciprocal of a radical, (2) as a power of 2, and (3) by a decimal approximation with 2 digits to the right of the decimal:

   (a) up 32 cents

   (b) down 750 cents

   (c) up a minor third

   (d) the interval from C_3 to $F_1^\sharp$

2. Assuming A_4 is tuned to 440 Hz, find the frequencies for all the notes of the chromatic scale from C_4 to C_5. Plot these points on a number line, noting their failure to be equidistant.

3. Suppose middle C is tuned as 256 Hz. (Note: This is not standard practice.) Find the frequencies for:

   (a) A_4 (b) $D_2^\sharp$ (c) C_3 (d) $F_1^\sharp$

4. Graph the function $f(x) = 2^{x/12}$. Explain the non-equidistance of the points plotted in Exercise 1 by observing the shape of this graph.

5. For each of the following chords, voiced within an octave with the root on the bottom, give the pitch of each note in the chord:

   (a) major triad with root C_3

   (b) minor triad with root $G^\sharp_4$

   (c) minor seventh chord with root A_5

   (d) diminished triad with root $B^\flat_4$

6. Suppose a string on a banjo has length 50 cm. Indicate positions of the 12 frets which will allow the string to play one octave of the ascending chromatic scale. Note the non-equidistance of adjacent frets.

7. On the banjo string described above, indicate positions of the frets which will allow the string to play one octave of the ascending 5-chromatic scale.

8. A string on a stringed instrument has length 100 cm. Indicate the positions of the single fret which will allow the string to play the note (a) a keyboard major third above the original pitch, and (b) a ratio 5/4 above the original pitch. (Note the closeness of these two positions, which relates to the discussion of Chapter 12.)

9. Determine whether each pair of interval ratios are equivalent modulo octave:

   (a) 5, 20   (b) 14, $\frac{7}{2}$ (c) 2.3, 9.2   (d) 1.04, 0.13   (e) π, $\frac{3\pi}{2}$

Chapter 5

Logarithms and Musical Intervals

The logarithm allows us to convert ratios into cents or semitones, which are the most natural representations of intervals. We will review some basic facts. In this discussion, b will be a positive real number $\neq 1$ which will serve as the *base* of the logarithm.

Exponents. If n is a positive integer, then b^n is the n-fold product $b \cdot b \cdots b$, $b^{-n} = 1/b^n$, and $b^{1/n} = \sqrt[n]{b}$. These facts, together with the rule of exponents

$$b^{st} = (b^s)^t,$$

give meaning to b^x for all rational numbers x. For example, $b^{-2/3}$ can be calculated as

$$b^{(-2) \cdot \left(\frac{1}{3}\right)} = (b^{-2})^{\frac{1}{3}} = \left(\frac{1}{b^2}\right)^{\frac{1}{3}} = \sqrt[3]{\frac{1}{b^2}}.$$

Exponential Functions. The calculus concept of limit provides a definition b^x for all real numbers x in such a way that $f(x) = b^x$ is a continuous function. (The concept of *continuity* will be discussed in Chapter 10.) Its domain is the set of real numbers $\mathbb{R}$ and (since $b \neq 1$) its range is the set of positive real numbers $\mathbb{R}^+$:

$$f : \mathbb{R} \to \mathbb{R}^+.$$

For $b > 1$ the function is increasing, hence it gives a one-to-one correspondence between the sets $\mathbb{R}$ and $\mathbb{R}^+$. The graph of $f(x) = b^x$ is given below.

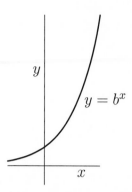

The number b is called the *base* of the exponential function. It will always be a positive real number, $\neq 1$, and we generally take it to be > 1.

Logarithmic Functions. Since the function $f(x)$ is one-to-one and onto, it has an inverse function. The function $g(x) = \log_b(x)$ is defined as the inverse function of $f(x) = b^x$, that is to say

$$f(g(x)) = x, \text{ which says } b^{\log_b x} = x,$$

and

$$g(f(x)) = x, \text{ which says } \log_b(b^x) = x.$$

Thus the statement $\log_b x = y$ means exactly the same as $b^y = x$. The domain of $g(x)$ (which is the range of $f(x)$) is $\mathbb{R}^+$; the range of $g(x)$ (which is the domain of $f(x)$) is $\mathbb{R}$:

$$g : \mathbb{R}^+ \to \mathbb{R}.$$

The graph of $g(x) = \log_b x$ is obtained by flipping the graph of $f(x) = b^x$ around the line $y = x$. Again assuming $b \geq 1$, we see that $g(x) = \log_b x$ is an increasing, hence one-to-one, function whose graph is:

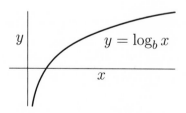

The number b is called the *base* of the logarithm. Remember that it is always positive, $\neq 1$, and we usually take it to be > 1.

If we recognize a number x as a power of b, then we can say immediately what $\log_b x$ is. For example, $\log_3 9 = 2$ (since $3^2 = 9$) and $\log_b \sqrt{b} = \frac{1}{2}$ (since $b^{\frac{1}{2}} = \sqrt{b}$).

Properties of Logarithms. In a certain sense, logarithms transform multiplication to addition; this is why they are useful in understanding and measuring intervals. The basic properties which underlie this are:

$$\boxed{\log_b xy = \log_b x + \log_b y} \qquad (\text{L1})$$

$$\boxed{\log_b \frac{x}{y} = \log_b x - \log_b y} \qquad (\text{L2})$$

$$\boxed{\log_b(x^p) = p \log_b x} \qquad (\text{L3})$$

for any real numbers $x, y > 0$ and any real number p. Property (L1) derives from the law of exponents $b^{s+t} = b^s b^t$ as follows: Let $s = \log_b x$ and $t = \log_b y$. Then

$$b^{s+t} = b^s b^t = b^{\log_b x} b^{\log_b y} = xy,$$

according to the above principle. But $b^{s+t} = xy$ means $s + t = \log_b xy$, completing the proof.

Logarithmic Scale for Pitch. Property (L2) assures us a pleasing outcome if we plot pitches on an axis corresponding to the *logarithm* of their frequency: Pairs of pitches which have the same interval will lie the same distance apart on the axis. For suppose pitches (i.e., frequencies) x and y create the same interval as the two x' and y'. This means the ratio of the frequencies is the same, i.e., $x/y = x'/y'$. According to (L2), then, we have $\log_b x - \log_b y = \log_b x' - \log_b y'$, which says the distance between $\log_b x$ and $\log_b y$ is the same as the distance between $\log_b x'$ and $\log_b y'$. Recall that when we plot A_2, A_3, A_4, and A_5 according to their frequencies we get:

	A_2	A_3	A_4		A_5
0	110	220	440		880

If we instead plot these notes according to the logarithm of their frequencies we find that they are equally spaced. For example, choosing $b = 10$, we get:

A_2	A_3	A_4	A_5
$\log_{10} 110$	$\log_{10} 220$	$\log_{10} 440$	$\log_{10} 880$
≈ 2.041	≈ 2.342	≈ 2.643	≈ 2.944

Different Bases. We will need to compare logarithms of different bases. If a is another positive number $\neq 1$, we have the following relationship between $\log_b x$ and $\log_a x$:

$$\boxed{\log_b x = \frac{\log_a x}{\log_a b}} \tag{L4}$$

This is established as follows. Let $u = \log_a x$, $v = \log_b x$, and $w = \log_a b$. Then $a^u = x$, $b^v = x$, and $a^w = b$. The last two equations give us $x = (a^w)^v = a^{wv}$. This establishes that $wv = \log_a x = u$ from which (L4) is immediate.

The result is that the functions $\log_b x$ and $\log_a x$ are proportional as functions, with constant of proportionality $1/\log_a b$. For example, if we compare the graphs of $g(x) = \log_6 x$ and $\log_3 x$ we see that the latter is obtained by "stretching" the former vertically by a factor of $\log_3 6 \approx 1.631$.

Calculating Using the Natural Logarithm. Scientists often prefer to use the *natural logarithm*, which has as its base the transcendental number e, approximated by 2.71828. This number and its logarithm are highly significant in mathematics for reasons that will not be explained here. It is common to denote $\log_e x$ by $\ln x$. Any calculator that has ln as a supplied function can be used to evaluate any logarithm, using (L4). Setting $a = e$ the formula reads:

$$\boxed{\log_b x = \frac{\ln x}{\ln b}} \tag{L5}$$

Similarly, one can calculate any logarithm using $\log_{10}$, which is supplied with many calculators.

Converting Intervals from Multiplicative to Additive Measurement. Suppose we want the octave interval to appear as the distance 1 on the logarithmic axis. If two frequencies x and y are an octave apart, x being the greater frequency, then we know $x/y = 2$. We need, then, $1 = \log_b x - \log_b y = \log_b(x/y) = \log_b 2$. But $\log_b 2 = 1$ means $b^1 = 2$, i.e., $b = 2$. Therefore 2 is our desired base.

Returning to a problem posed in the last section, suppose we are given a musical interval represented as a ratio r and we wish to convert it to one of the standard measurements for intervals such as octaves, steps, semitones, or cents. We have noted that if x is the measurement of the interval in cents, then $r = 2^{x/1200}$. Applying the function $\log_2$ to both sides of this equation yields $\log_2 r = \log_2(2^{x/1200}) = x/1200$, i.e., $x = 1200 \log_2 r$. Thus we have:

$$\boxed{\text{The interval ratio } r \text{ is measured in cents by } 1200 \log_2 r.} \tag{5.1}$$

Similar reasoning shows:

> The interval ratio r is measured in semitones by $12 \log_2 r$ (5.2)

and:

> The interval ratio r is measured in octaves by $\log_2 r$.   (5.3)

Using (L4) we can make these conversions using any base. For example, if our calculator only provides the natural logarithm, we appeal to (L5) to make the conversion by evaluating $x = 1200 \log_2 r$ as

$$x = 1200 \left(\frac{\ln r}{\ln 2} \right).$$

Note that if r is less than 1, then $\ln r < 0$, hence measurement x in cents is negative. This is logical, for if r is the interval from frequency f_1 to frequency f_2 we have $r = f_2/f_1 < 1$. This says f_2 is less than f_1, so that the interval in cents is given by a negative number.

We note that the conversions in (5.1) and (5.2) can be expressed as $\log_b r$ for an appropriate base b. For example, if we wish to express the ratio r as x semitones, we have

$$r = 2^{\frac{x}{12}} = \left(2^{\frac{1}{12}} \right)^x = \left(\sqrt[12]{2} \right)^x.$$

Applying $\log_b$ with $b = \sqrt[12]{2}$ we get

$$x = \log_{\sqrt[12]{2}} r.$$

Example. Let us measure in cents the interval given by the ratio $3/2$ and find the chromatic interval which best approximates this interval. If x is the measurement in cents, we have

$$
\begin{aligned}
x &= 1200 \left(\frac{\ln(3/2)}{\ln 2} \right) \\
&= 1200 \left(\frac{\ln 3 - \ln 2}{\ln 2} \right) \quad \text{by (L2)} \\
&= 1200 \left(\frac{\ln 3}{\ln 2} - 1 \right) \\
&\approx 701.955 \quad \text{using a calculator.}
\end{aligned}
$$

Thus the ratio $3/2$ is very close to 702 cents. A fifth is 700 cents ($= 7$ semitones), so our interval is 2 cents greater than a fifth. The fifth is the chromatic interval that gives the best approximation.

Exercises

1. Evaluate without a calculator by writing the argument of log as a power of the base. Write down each step of the simplification, e.g., $\log_3 3\sqrt{3} = \log_3 3^{3/2} = \frac{3}{2}\log_3 3 = \frac{3}{2}$:

   (a) $\log_{10}(0.01)$ (b) $\log_2 16$ (c) $\log_5 \sqrt[3]{25}$ (d) $\log_c \sqrt[n]{c^\ell}$

2. Express as a single logarithm without coefficient, i.e., in the form $\log_b c$ (do not evaluate with a calculator):

   (e) $\log_3 11 + \log_3 17$ (f) $\log_9 5 - 2\log_9 2$

   (g) $\log_2 13 + \log_4 21$ (h) $2\log_c x^2 - \frac{1}{2}\log_{\sqrt{c}} x$

3. Sketch the graphs of:

   (a) $f(x) = 10^x$ (b) $g(x) = \log_{10} x$ (c) $r(x) = 2^x$ (d) $s(x) = \log_2 x$

   Determine which pairs of these functions are inverse to each other, and which pairs differ by a horizontal or vertical stretch/compression. In the latter case, identify the stretch factor, justifying your answer.

4. For a base b with $0 < b < 1$, sketch the graph of $f(x) = b^x$ and $g(x) = \log_b x$ and explain what happens if we plot pitches according to the logarithm of their frequency using the base b.

5. Prove the properties of logarithms

$$\log_b \frac{x}{y} = \log_b x - \log_b y$$

   and

$$\log_b(x^p) = p\log_b x$$

   using properties of exponents.

6. Suppose $n \in \mathbb{Z}^+$ and we want the interval of an octave to correspond to a distance of n on the logarithmic axis. What base should we choose? Justify your answer.

7. Convert to semitones the intervals given by the following ratios, rounding off to 2 digits to the right of the decimal:

   (a) 3   (b) 0.8   (c) $\dfrac{4}{3}$ (d) $\sqrt[3]{2}$ (e) e

8. Convert to cents the intervals given by the following ratios, rounding off to the nearest whole cent:

   (a) 1.25   (b) 1.1   (c) $\dfrac{7}{4}$ (d) $\dfrac{2}{3}$ (e) π

9. Write on the staff the note which best approximates the frequency having the given interval ratio r from the given note:

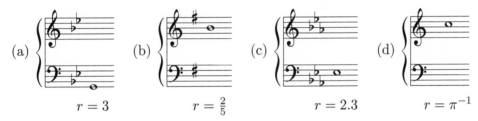

(a) $r = 3$ (b) $r = \frac{2}{5}$ (c) $r = 2.3$ (d) $r = \pi^{-1}$

10. Express the following interval ratios in terms of n-chromatic units, for the given n, rounding off to 2 digits to the right of the decimal:

    (a) ratio $\frac{5}{2}$; $n = 19$

    (b) ratio 3 ; $n = 8$

    (c) ratio 0.85 ; $n = 13$

    (d) ratio 2π ; $n = 4$ (i.e., minor thirds)

11. For the values $n = 11, 17, 21, 30$, find the n-chromatic scale's best approximation of the interval ratio $3/2$, and calculate the error in cents. Which of these values of n gives the best approximation, and is that approximation as good as that of the 12-chromatic scale?

Chapter 6

Chromatic Scales

As we have seen, the interval of an octave is given by a two-to-one ratio of frequencies. Two pitches an octave apart, played simultaneously, present the ear with a two-against-one pattern that the brain easily recognizes as a pleasing consonance. Therefore it is easy to understand what led Western music, as well as other musical traditions, to embrace the octave and to incorporate octave identification into its notation.

What is not so apparent is what led to the subdivision of the octave into twelve equal intervals, a custom which is less universal, and which only came into acceptance within the last 200 years. It is quite natural to wonder if the subdivision of the octave into 12 equal intervals is purely arbitrary, or if some natural phenomenon brought Western music toward this practice. This will be discussed later.

Meanwhile, we can explore the sound of chromatic scales that equally divide the octave differently. For example we might want to design and listen to a chromatic scale which divides the octave into 19, 10, or 5 equal intervals.

Non-Standard Chromatic Scales. If we obtain a chromatic unit by dividing the octave into n equal intervals, where n is a positive integer, this unit measured as a ratio is $2^{\frac{1}{n}}$, and measured in cents is $1200/n$. We will refer to the resulting chromatic scale as the *n-chromatic scale,* and the smallest chromatic interval ($= \frac{1}{n}$ octaves) as the *n-chromatic unit.* Thus the 12-chromatic unit is the usual semitone. The n-chromatic unit is measured in cents by $1200/n$ and has interval ratio $\sqrt[n]{2}$.

Detuning. Many synthesizers allow notes of the chromatic scale to be individually detuned in cents, and this feature will allow one to experience the sound of such non-standard chromatic scales where $n < 12$.

If we choose $n = 4$ the smallest interval will be $1200/4 = 300$ cents, which is the keyboard's minor third. So the scale can be played on a keyboard without detuning. For example, in G we would play G, $B^\flat$, $D^\flat$, and E. For $n = 3$ the smallest chromatic interval would be the major third, and for $n = 6$ it would be the (whole) step.

If we choose $n = 5$, some detuning is required. We could detune the notes A, B, C, D so that the five keys G, A, B, C, D play the five-note chromatic scale. The interval in cents would be $1200/5 = 240$. We need the interval between G and A to be 240. The default interval is one step, or 200 cents, so A should be detuned upward by 40 cents. B needs to be 240 cents above the detuned A, so B should be detuned upward by 80 cents. C, which by default is only 100 cents above the default B, will need to be detuned upward by 220 cents. Detuning D upward by 260 cents completes the task. With this accomplished, and using only these five keys, we can listen to the sound of the five-note chromatic scale and experiment with melody and harmony in this tuning environment.

Generating Intervals. We now give a brief preview of a topic that will be reintroduced and developed in Chapters 7 and 8. For a fixed positive integer n, the *generating intervals* are those modular n-chromatic intervals I for which all modular n-chromatic intervals can be expressed as iterations of I. We will see later that the generating intervals correspond to those $[m] \in \mathbb{Z}_n$ which are generators for the group $\mathbb{Z}_n$, which, it will be shown, is equivalent to saying $\gcd(m, n) = 1$. This denotes the *greatest common divisor* of m and n, to be discussed in Chapter 8. It is defined as the largest possible integer which divides both m and n. Two numbers m and n are called *relatively prime* (to each other) if $\gcd(m, n) = 1$. In number theory, the *Euler phi function* ϕ is defined as the function from $\phi : \mathbb{Z}^+ \to \mathbb{Z}^+$ which takes n to the number of integers $m < n$ in $\mathbb{Z}^+$ such that $\gcd(m, n) = 1$. Thus $\phi(n)$ also counts the generating intervals in the equally tempered n-scale. For any such I the "circle" based on I (the meaning of this will become clear in the example below) contains all intervals in the chromatic scale.

Example. Consider the case $n = 14$. The numbers 1, 3, 5, 9, 11, and 13 are the positive integers < 14 which are relatively prime to 14, so $\phi(14) = 6$. These six numbers, modulo 14, give the six generating intervals in the 14-chromatic scale. For the interval I corresponding to [5], its circle of intervals is the following.

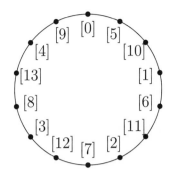

Approximating Standard Keyboard Intervals. Let us determine how closely some of the standard intervals of the standard 12-chromatic scale's intervals can be approximated using the 14-chromatic scale. Clearly the tritone is precisely 7 chromatic units in the 14-scale, being one-half of an octave. More generally, ℓ semitones can be calculated by:

$$\ell \text{ semitones} = \ell \cdot \frac{14 \text{ 14-chromatic units}}{12 \text{ semitones}} = \tfrac{7}{6}\ell \text{ 14-chromatic units.}$$

For example, the keyboard's interval of a fourth, being 5 semitones, is $\left(\tfrac{7}{6}\right) \cdot 5 = \tfrac{35}{6} \approx 5.833$ 14-chromatic units. Hence it is best approximated in the 14-scale by 6 units. Now, since the chromatic unit is $(1/14)$-th of an octave, it is measured in cents by $1200/14 \approx 85.714$. Therefore 6 units is $6 \cdot (1200/14) \approx 514.29$ cents, which is 14.29 cents greater than the fourth.

To calculate a ratio r in 14-chromatic units, we reason as follows: A 14-chromatic unit has ratio $2^{\frac{1}{14}} = \sqrt[14]{2}$. If x is the measurement of r in 14-chromatic units, then $r = (\sqrt[14]{2})^x = 2^{\frac{x}{14}}$. Solving for x using the logarithm, we have

$$x = 14 \log_2 r = 14 \frac{\ln r}{\ln 2}.$$

For example, the ratio 0.75 is $14 \ln(0.75)/\ln 2 \approx -5.81$ chromatic units (i.e., 5.81 units downward).

Twelve-Tone Music. In the 1920s Arnold Schoenberg (1874-1951) began developing the twelve-tone technique of composition, a method that is heavily based on the subdivision of the octave into 12 equal units. It was continued by Anton Webern (1883-1945), Alban Berg (1885-1935), and Milton Babbitt (b.1916). Here consonance is largely abandoned in favor of combinatorics. This represents a type of *serial music*, which constructs music from sets of note classes. The reader is referred to Chapter 2 of [3], which gives an excellent exposition on methods of twelve-tone composing, and from which the twelve-tone examples which follow are taken.

A twelve-tone composition is based on a *row chart,* which is a 12 by 12 array having the following properties: Each entry is one of the 12 note classes, modulo octave. Each row and each column contains each note class precisely once. All entries are obtained from the top row, called the *original row,* or *prime row,* as follows. The leftmost column is the *inversion* of the top row, that is, the interval (modulo octave) from the top left note class to the n-th entry in the left column is the opposite of the interval from the top left note class to the n-th entry in the top row. The subsequent rows are *transpositions* of the top row; they are filled in by starting with the left entry that has been provided above and transposing the first row, so the the intervals from entry 1 to entry m in the n-th row is the same as the interval from entry 1 to entry m in the first row.

When we are finished, the columns will be transpositions of the inversion of the original row, or, equivalently, inversions of the various transpositions of the original row. The reason for this outcome is fairly obvious, but we will see precisely why this happens when we make the connection with modular arithmetic in the next chapter.

The number of possible original rows is

$$12! = 12 \cdot 11 \cdot 10 \cdot 9 \cdot 8 \cdot 7 \cdot 6 \cdot 5 \cdot 4 \cdot 3 \cdot 2 \cdot 1,$$

a number huge enough to make the possibilities seemingly endless.

As an example, consider this sequence of 12 note classes:

The spelling of notes in twelve-tone music often consists of a mixture of sharps and flats in no apparent pattern. Observe in the above that the sharp is used four times and the flat one time. Since each of the 12 note classes appears precisely once, this sequence qualifies as an original (top) row, which generates the row chart below.

E	G	F♯	A	G♯	C	F	D	D♯	C♯	B	B♭
C♯	E	D♯	F♯	F	A	D	B	C	B♭	G♯	G
D	F	E	G	F♯	B♭	D♯	C	C♯	B	A	G♯
B	D	C♯	E	D♯	G	C	A	B♭	G♯	F♯	F
C	D♯	D	F	E	G♯	C♯	B♭	B	A	G	F♯
G♯	B	B♭	C♯	C	E	A	F♯	G	F	D♯	D
D♯	F♯	F	G♯	G	B	E	C♯	D	C	B♭	A
F♯	A	G♯	B	B♭	D	G	E	F	D♯	C♯	C
F	G♯	G	B♭	A	C♯	F♯	D♯	E	D	C	B
G	B♭	A	C	B	D♯	G♯	F	F♯	E	D	C♯
A	C	B	D	C♯	F	B♭	G	G♯	F♯	E	D♯
B♭	C♯	C	D♯	D	F♯	B	G♯	A	G	F	E

The goal of twelve-tone composing is to create a musical composition which uses the sequences of note classes found in the rows and/or columns, or by taking their *retrogrades,* which reverse the order of the sequences. The retrogrades are obtained by reading the rows from right to left or the columns from bottom to top.

The following example, from [3], is based on the row chart above.

Note that the sequence of notes in the bass clef is the original row, the top line in the treble clef is the retrograde of the original row, and the bottom line in the treble clef is the second column of the row chart, which is a transposition of the inversion. The sequences from the row chart are applied horizontally in the music, often producing the clashing effect of dissonant chords.

Since there is little feeling of tonal center, twelve-tone music is often written in the key of C. The spelling may be different from what appears in the row chart (observe the A^b, rather than $G^\sharp$, in the above example), and they may change during the composition.

Sometimes the notes from a sequence are assembled in vertical fashion. Consider the following original row.

$$\text{C} \quad \text{A}^b \quad \text{D} \quad \text{F} \quad \text{A} \quad \text{C}^\sharp \quad \text{E} \quad \text{E}^b \quad \text{B}^b \quad \text{B} \quad \text{G} \quad \text{F}^\sharp$$

The following example, again from [3], uses this row by using groups of note classes vertically.

Exercises

1. Which interval in the given n-chromatic scale best approximates the given keyboard interval? Express the interval in n-chromatic units.

    (a) 19-scale, major third

    (b) 48-scale, tritone

    (c) 37-scale, step

    (d) 7-scale, down a major sixth

2. Express the following interval ratios in terms of n-chromatic units, for the given n. Round off to 2 digits to the right of the decimal.

    (a) ratio $\frac{5}{2}$; $n = 19$

    (b) ratio 3; $n = 8$

    (c) ratio 0.85; $n = 13$

    (d) ratio 2π; $n = 4$ (i.e., the chromatic scale of minor thirds)

3. Identify the following chords by root note with suffix (e.g., $B\,m^7$) <u>and</u> root scale note with suffix (e.g., V^7). Indicate the chromatic n-scale's best approximation of the chord by giving, for each note in the chord, its interval in (whole) n-chromatic units from the bottom note.

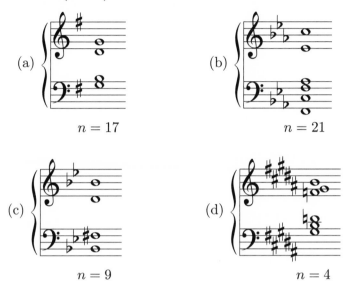

(a) $n = 17$

(b) $n = 21$

(c) $n = 9$

(d) $n = 4$

4. Create a twelve-tone row chart having this sequence as its original row:

Write a short composition (say, ≤ 3 bars) which uses only the retrograde of the original row's inversion (i.e., the left column of the chart read from bottom to top), incorporating some harmonic material.

Chapter 7

Octave Identification and Modular Arithmetic

Octave Identification. As we pointed out before, musical notation often implicitly equates notes which differ by an interval of m octaves, where m is an integer. In this scenario, the chromatic scale contains all the notes of standard musical notation, of which there are twelve. Starting from C, we can number them 0 through 11 as follows:

(0) C

(1) $C^\sharp = D^\flat$

(2) D

(3) $D^\sharp = E^\flat$

(4) E

(5) F

(6) $F^\sharp = G^\flat$

(7) G

(8) $G^\sharp = A^\flat$

(9) A

(10) $A^\sharp = B^\flat$

(11) B

(Of course, there are other enharmonic representations of the note classes listed above, such as F = E$^\sharp$ and A = B$^{\flat\flat}$.)

Similarly, we identify intervals which differ by m octaves, for some integer m. From this perspective, going up an octave is the same as the identity interval. Hence the interval of a fourth followed by the interval of a fifth yields the unison interval. Likewise going up two fifths is the same as going up one step. In this way intervals created between notes in the chromatic scale (i.e., those which can be measured as whole multiples of a semitone) are parameterized by the modular group $\mathbb{Z}_{12}$ and iterating intervals amounts to adding or subtracting in this algebraic system. We will now investigate this phenomenon.

Variations on the Well-Ordering Principle. We will shortly give a proof which will appeal to the Well-Ordering Principle, which we take to be an axiom. We state four different formulations of that principle, which are easily seen to be equivalent. The first is precisely as it was stated in Chapter 1. In the second formulation, $\mathbb{Z}^-$ denotes the set of strictly negative integers. A real number y is called a *lower bound* for a set of numbers T if $y \leq t$ for all $t \in T$. The definition of *upper bound* is analogous.

WOP 1. *Any non-empty subset of $\mathbb{Z}^+$ has a smallest element.*

WOP 2. *Any non-empty subset of $\mathbb{Z}^-$ has a largest element.*

WOP 3. *Any non-empty subset of $\mathbb{Z}$ which has a lower bound has a smallest element.*

WOP 4. *Any non-empty subset of $\mathbb{Z}$ which has an upper bound has a largest element.*

Generalized Division Algorithm. We now state a more general version of the Division Algorithm than the one presented in Chapter 1. Note the generality is that we allow the "dividend" x to be any real number rather than an integer.[1]

GENERALIZED DIVISION ALGORITHM. *Given $m \in \mathbb{Z}^+$ and $x \in \mathbb{R}$ there exist $q \in \mathbb{Z}$ and $r \in \mathbb{R}$ with*

$$0 \leq r < m \tag{7.1}$$

---

[1]Actually, you can see from the proof that the "divisor" m in the algorithm can be any element of $\mathbb{R}^+$, not just a positive integer.

such that

$$x = qm + r. \tag{7.2}$$

The elements $q \in \mathbb{Z}$ and $r \in \mathbb{R}$ are uniquely determined by (7.1) and (7.2).

Proof. Consider the set

$$S = \{\ell \in \mathbb{Z} \mid \ell m \leq x\} \subset \mathbb{Z}.$$

The condition $\ell m \leq x$ is equivalent to $\ell \leq \frac{x}{m}$ (since m is positive), so we see that x/m is an upper bound for S. By the Well-Ordering Principle (WOP 4 above), S has a largest element q. We must have $q+1 \notin S$ by the maximality of q and hence we have

$$qm \leq x < (q+1)m = qm + m. \tag{7.3}$$

Setting $r = x - qm$, we clearly have $x = qm + r$, and subtracting qm from (7.3) gives $0 \leq r < m$ as desired.

As for the uniqueness of q and r, suppose we have $q' \in \mathbb{Z}$, $r' \in \mathbb{R}$ such that $x = q'm + r'$ and $0 \leq r' < m$. Note that $q'm = x - r' \leq x$ so $q' \in S$. Since $r' < m$ we have $x = q'm + r' < q'm + m = (q' + 1)m$. The inequality $(q' + 1)m > x$ shows that $q' + 1 \notin S$, nor is any larger integer. Therefore q' is the largest element of S, hence $q' = q$. We now have $qm + r' = qm + r$ since both are equal to x. Subtracting qm yields $r' = r$. $\square$

Modular Equivalence on the Real Numbers. Let m be a fixed positive integer. We declare two real numbers x and y to be equivalent if $k - \ell$ is a multiple of m in $\mathbb{Z}$, i.e., there exists $q \in \mathbb{Z}$ such that $x - y = qm$, or equivalently $x = y + qm$. This relationship is denoted by $x \sim y$. Note that this depends on the choice of m.

We leave as an exercise the proof that $\sim$ defines an equivalence relation on the set $\mathbb{R}$, hence it partitions $\mathbb{R}$ into equivalence classes. For $x \in \mathbb{R}$ let us denote by $\bar{x}$ the equivalence class of x. Thus, if $m = 8$, we have $\overline{13} = \overline{53} = \overline{-11}$ and $\overline{6.5} = \overline{-1.5}$.

Let us denote the set of equivalence classes by $\mathbb{R}/\sim$. The function which associates to $x \in \mathbb{R}$ its equivalence class $\bar{x} \in \mathbb{R}/\sim$ can be seen as the function that wraps the number line around the circle of circumference m in such a way that distance is preserved as arc length. We often do this so that the origin $x = 0$ goes to the point at the top of the circle. This is depicted below for the case $m = 8$.

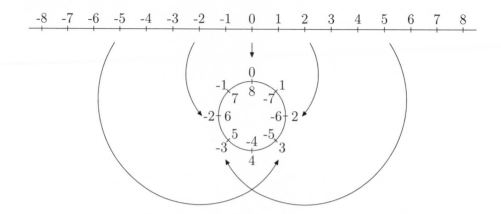

Thus $\mathbb{R}/\sim$ is parameterized by the circle in the same way $\mathbb{R}$ is parameterized by the line.

The Generalized Division Algorithm asserts that for each $x \in \mathbb{R}$, there is precisely one equivalence class representative $r \in \bar{x}$ such that $0 \leq r < m$. It is the number r for which $x = qm + r$ in the algorithm. This is reflected in the fact that for any point p on the circle there is precisely one point in the interval $[0, m)$ which wraps onto p.

Modular Equivalence on the Integers. Note that if $x \sim y$ and if $x \in \mathbb{Z}$, then $y \in \mathbb{Z}$ as well. Therefore $\sim$ restricts to an equivalence relation on $\mathbb{Z}$ as well. We denote by $\mathbb{Z}_m$ the set of equivalence classes. Elements of $\mathbb{Z}_m$ are called *modular integers*. For $k, \ell \in \mathbb{Z}$ we express the condition $k \sim \ell$ as

$$k \cong \ell \mod m.$$

For $k \in \mathbb{Z}$, we write $[k]$ for the equivalence class containing k. Note that the symbol $[\ ]$ does not reference m, so again m must always be established. Bear in mind that $[k] = [\ell]$ if and only if $m \mid k - \ell$ in $\mathbb{Z}$. As an example, note that $5 \equiv 19 \mod 7$, and hence $[5] = [19]$ in $\mathbb{Z}_7$.

The set $\mathbb{Z}_m$ is a subset of $\mathbb{R}/\sim$, and it can be seen as the image of $\mathbb{Z}$ by the wrapping function described above. If we place m equally spaced points around the circle, these points will be this image; they correspond to the classes $[0], [1], [2], \ldots, [m-1]$, which is all of $\mathbb{Z}_m$. Hence elements of $\mathbb{Z}_m$ can be seen as "clock positions" on the "m-hour clock". This is depicted below, again for $m = 8$.

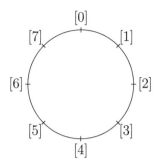

We now introduce some concepts from abstract algebra which will be useful in this discussion.

Monoid. A *monoid* is a set M with an associative law of composition that has an identity element. By "law of composition" we mean a rule which assigns to each ordered pair of elements $(x, y) \in M^2$ an element z of M. This operation is often denoted by choosing some symbol, such as $\cdot$, and writing $x \cdot y = z$. The property of associativity and the existence of an identity element are defined as follows:

(1) Associativity: For any $x, y, z \in M$ we have $(x \cdot y) \cdot z = x \cdot (y \cdot z)$.

(2) Identity: There exists an element $e \in M$, called the *identity element,* having the property that for all $x \in M$, $x \cdot e = e \cdot x = x$.

Note that the associative property allows us to drop parentheses without ambiguity: $(x \cdot y) \cdot z = x \cdot (y \cdot z)$ can be written as $x \cdot y \cdot z$.

We claim that the identity element e is the unique element of M having its defining property, justifying our use of the article "the". For if e' is another identity element, then $e = e \cdot e' = e'$.

Examples. Here are some examples of monoids. We leave it as an exercise to verify most of the details.

(a) The set $\mathbb{R}$ under the operation $\cdot$ (ordinary multiplication).

(b) The set $\mathbb{Z}$ together with the operation $+$ (addition). The identity element is 0.

(c) Let S be a set and let $\mathcal{F}(S)$ be the set of functions $f : S \to S$. Take the law of composition to be the usual composition of functions: For $f, g \in \mathcal{F}(S)$, $f \circ g$ is the function defined by $(f \circ g)(s) = f(g(s))$ for all $s \in S$. The identity element is the "identity function" id_S defined by $\mathrm{id}_S(s) = s$ for all $s \in S$. A special case is $\mathcal{F}(\mathbb{R})$, the monoid of functions from $\mathbb{R}$ to $\mathbb{R}$.

(d) The set $\mathbb{Z}_m$, for a given $m \in \mathbb{Z}^+$. The law of composition will be denoted $+$ (we'll call it addition), and defined by

$$[k] + [\ell] = [k + \ell].$$

Here we must show that this is well defined, due to the fact that we have defined the addition using equivalence class representatives. Suppose then that $[k'] = [k]$ and $[\ell'] = [\ell]$. This means $k' \equiv k \mod m$ and $\ell' \equiv \ell \mod m$. Hence we have $k' = k + pm$ and $\ell' = \ell + qm$ for some $p, q \in \mathbb{Z}$. Therefore $k' + \ell' = (k + pm) + (\ell + qm) = k + \ell + (p+q)m$, which shows $k' + \ell' \equiv k + \ell \mod m$. This means $[k' + \ell'] = [k + \ell]$, and this shows that our definition is well defined. Note that the identity element is $[0]$.

We sometimes denote a monoid by writing $(M, \cdot)$ to indicate its law of composition. This is necessary when the intended operation is not clear in the context. For example $(\mathbb{Z}, +)$ and $(\mathbb{Z}, \cdot)$ are two different monoid structures having the same underlying set.

Note that a monoid is always a non-empty set, since it contains the element e.

Commutativity. A monoid M is called *commutative* if for all $x, y \in M$ we have $x \cdot y = y \cdot x$.

One will easily verify that the monoids defined in (a), (b), and (d) above are commutative. However, example (c) is not, in general: consider for example the functions $f, g \in \mathcal{F}(\mathbb{R})$ given by $f(x) = x^2$ and $g(x) = x + 1$. Then $(f \circ g)(x) = (x + 1)^2$ and $(g \circ f)(x) = x^2 + 1$. These two are not the same function; they differ at $x = 1$, for example.

By convention, we only use the symbol $+$ for commutative operations.

Group. A *group* is a monoid G with the following property: For every $x \in G$ there is an element x_{inv}, called the *inverse* of x, with the property

$$x \cdot x_{\mathrm{inv}} = x_{\mathrm{inv}} \cdot x = e$$

(where e is the identity element).

The inverse x_{inv} is easily shown to be unique to x. If x'_{inv} were another such element we have

$$x_{\text{inv}} = x_{\text{inv}} \cdot e = x_{\text{inv}} \cdot (x \cdot x'_{\text{inv}}) = (x_{\text{inv}} \cdot x) \cdot x'_{\text{inv}} = e \cdot x'_{\text{inv}} = x'_{\text{inv}}.$$

When we are using the symbol $+$ for the law of composition in a commutative group, we denote the inverse of an element x by $-x$, and we write $x - y$ for $x + (-y)$.

Examples. Amongst the examples (a) – (d) above of monoids, note that (b) and (d) are groups: The inverse of $k \in \mathbb{Z}$ is $-k$, and the inverse of $[k] \in \mathbb{Z}_m$ is $[-k]$. Example (a) fails since $0 \in \mathbb{R}$ has no multiplicative inverse. However, if we replace $\mathbb{R}$ by either $\mathbb{R} - \{0\}$ or $\mathbb{R}^+$ we have a group, where the inverse of x is $\frac{1}{x} = x^{-1}$.

Modular Arithmetic. The group $\mathbb{Z}_m$ is called a *modular group*, and operations involving its law of composition, such as $[6] + [13] = [1]$ in $\mathbb{Z}_9$, are called *modular arithmetic*.

Homomorphism. Suppose we have two groups $(G, \cdot)$ and $(G', \circ)$. A function $\varphi : G \to G'$ is called a group *homomorphism* if for all $x, y \in G$ we have

$$\varphi(x \cdot y) = \varphi(x) \circ \varphi(y).$$

We leave it as an exercise to show that if $e \in G$ and $e' \in G'$ are the identity elements and φ is a homomorphism, then $\varphi(e) = e'$.

A homomorphism $\varphi : G \to G'$ is called an *isomorphism* if it is bijective, i.e., one-to-one and onto. In this case there is an inverse function $\varphi^{-1} : G' \to G$, and φ^{-1} will be an isomorphism as well. If such an isomorphism exists we say G and G' are *isomorphic*.

Examples.

(1) Let S be the set $\{\pm 1\} \subset \mathbb{R}$, multiplication. This is a group. The function $\varphi : S \to \mathbb{Z}_m$ defined by $\varphi(1) = [0]$, $\varphi(-1) = [1]$ is a homomorphism and, in fact, an isomorphism.

(2) Consider the function discussed earlier which wraps the real line around the circle. This is the function $w : \mathbb{R} \to \mathbb{R}/\sim$ defined by $w(x) = \bar{x}$. The set $\mathbb{R}/\sim$ inherits from $\mathbb{R}$ the law of composition $+$, by which $\bar{x} + \bar{y} = \overline{x + y}$. (One shows this is well defined by a proof analogous to the proof in (d) that addition is well defined in $\mathbb{Z}_m$.) Thus we have

groups $(\mathbb{R}, +)$ and $(\mathbb{R}/\sim, +)$, and the function w is a group homomorphism. This homomorphism is onto but not one-to-one, hence it is not an isomorphism.

(3) For $b \in \mathbb{R}^+$, we have encountered the functions $f : \mathbb{R} \to \mathbb{R}^+$ and $g : \mathbb{R}^+ \to \mathbb{R}$ defined by $fr = b^r$ and $g(x) = \log_b x$. These are homomorphisms between the groups $(\mathbb{R}, +)$ and $(\mathbb{R}^+, \cdot)$, which are inverse to each other as functions. Hence these two groups are isomorphic. The details are left as an exercise.

The Group of Intervals. The latter example is especially relevant since we have identified the set of musical intervals with the sets $\mathbb{R}$ and $\mathbb{R}^+$, the former giving additive measurement (the units depending on the base b), the latter giving multiplicative measurement, or interval ratio. We see by either identification the set of intervals forms a group, where the law of composition is the usual composition of intervals, i.e., following one interval by the other. We see, then, that the identity element in the group of intervals is the unison interval and the inverse of an interval is its opposite interval. The isomorphisms f and g are precisely the conversion from multiplicative to additive measurement, and back.

The Group of Modular Intervals. Elements of the group $(\mathbb{R}/\sim, +)$ in example (2) can be identified with the set of equivalence classes of intervals modulo octave. Thus the set of these classes becomes a group, which we'll call the group of *modular intervals*. The law of composition is defined by taking representatives, adding them, and taking the class of the sum. Thus we have, for example, third + ninth = tritone and fourth + fifth = unison.

The Group of Modular Chromatic Intervals. We have noted that the set of keyboard intervals, measured in semitones, can be identified with the group $\mathbb{Z}$. Let us note that the equivalence relation which says intervals of k and ℓ semitones are octave equivalent is just the statement that $k - \ell$ is a multiple of 12, i.e., $k \equiv \ell \mod 12$. We will call equivalence classes *modular chromatic intervals*. Therefore the set of modular chromatic intervals can be identified with $\mathbb{Z}_{12}$, making it a group whose law of composition is given by composition of intervals. Any modular chromatic interval has a unique equivalence class representative n semitones, where $0 \le n \le 11$. As with performing addition in $\mathbb{Z}_{12}$, the iteration of modular chromatic intervals can be seen as a sequence of rotations on the modular clock.

Example. Consider the composition of a minor third, an octave, and a fourth. These intervals are represented in semitones as 3, 12, and 5, respectively. However the octave can be represented by 0 semitones. The composition of the three intervals yields the modular chromatic interval represented by 8 semitones, which is an augmented fifth. This is merely the statement that $[3] + [12] + [5] = [8]$ in $\mathbb{Z}_{12}$, which follows from the fact that $20 \equiv 8$ mod 12.

Non-Standard Chromatic Intervals. If we divide the octave into n equal intervals and measure intervals by n-chromatic units, the group of intervals is identified with $\mathbb{Z}_n$.

Modular Clock. The group $\mathbb{Z}_n$ can be realized as the group of rotations of a regular n-gon, or of a "clock" with n positions, dividing the circle into n equal arcs, with a position at the top of the circle. For example, $\mathbb{Z}_4$ is the group of rotations of the square, or a clock with four positions:

We label a clock position by the group element which rotates the top position to that position. Hence the top position is labeled $[0]$, the first position clockwise from $[0]$ is labeled $[1]$, etc. The positions of the clock are thereby in one-to-one correspondence with the elements of $\mathbb{Z}_n$. With this labeling the addition of elements $[k]$ and $[\ell]$ in $\mathbb{Z}_n$ can be computed by rotating the clock clockwise by k positions (counter-clockwise if k is negative), then by ℓ positions. The sum $[k] + [\ell]$ will be where the top position lands after these two rotations.

Creating a Twelve-Tone Row Chart Using Modular Arithmetic. We can generate a twelve-tone row by designating a note class, then identifying each of the twelve note classes of the row with its modular chromatic interval from the designated note class. This just means we list the elements of $\mathbb{Z}_{12}$ in some order. For what is to follow it will be important to let the designated note be the first note class of the sequence, so that the first modular integer is $[0]$.

Example. We revisit the first example in Chapter 5, which generates the row chart whose original row is given below.

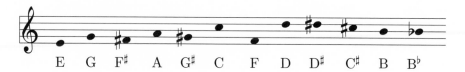

$$\text{E} \quad \text{G} \quad \text{F}^\sharp \quad \text{A} \quad \text{G}^\sharp \quad \text{C} \quad \text{F} \quad \text{D} \quad \text{D}^\sharp \quad \text{C}^\sharp \quad \text{B} \quad \text{B}^\flat$$

As prescribed above, let E be our designated note class. The sequence, given according to the modular interval from E, is then:

$$[0] \quad [3] \quad [2] \quad [5] \quad [4] \quad [8] \quad [1] \quad [10] \quad [11] \quad [9] \quad [7] \quad [6]$$

Provided our sequence starts with $[0]$, the inversion of this row is obtained by replacing each entry in the sequence by its additive inverse, or negative. This is because we want the interval from the first entry to the n-th entry in the inversion to be the opposite of the interval from the first entry to the n-th entry in the original row. Hence the sequence of intervals for the inversion of our given row is:

$$[0] \quad [9] \quad [10] \quad [7] \quad [8] \quad [4] \quad [11] \quad [2] \quad [1] \quad [3] \quad [5] \quad [6]$$

Let us number the rows and columns by the integers 1 through 12 and use the ordered pair (i, j) to refer to the position at row i and column j. We label the entries of the original row as:

$$a_1 = [0] \qquad a_2 = [3] \qquad a_3 = [2] \qquad a_4 = [5] \qquad a_5 = [4] \qquad a_6 = [8]$$
$$a_7 = [1] \qquad a_8 = [10] \qquad a_9 = [11] \qquad a_{10} = [9] \qquad a_{11} = [7] \qquad a_{12} = [6]$$

The first column will be the inversion, given by the negatives in $\mathbb{Z}_{12}$:

$$-a_1 = [0] \quad -a_2 = [9] \quad -a_3 = [10] \quad -a_4 = [7] \quad -a_5 = [8] \quad -a_6 = [4]$$
$$-a_7 = [11] \quad -a_8 = [2] \quad -a_9 = [1] \quad -a_{10} = [3] \quad -a_{11} = [5] \quad -a_{12} = [6]$$

We now proceed to fill in each position of the chart with the element of $\mathbb{Z}_{12}$ corresponding to the appropriate note class. According to the procedure described in Chapter 5, the entry in the (i, j) position should make the interval a_j with the leftmost entry in the i-th row, which is $-a_i$. Therefore the correct element of $\mathbb{Z}_{12}$ is $a_j - a_i$. For example, the entry in position $(8, 5)$ is $a_5 - a_8 = [4] - [10] = [6]$. Filling in the chart in this fashion yields the following row chart.

	1	2	3	4	5	6	7	8	9	10	11	12
1	[0]	[3]	[2]	[5]	[4]	[8]	[1]	[10]	[11]	[9]	[7]	[6]
2	[9]	[0]	[11]	[2]	[1]	[5]	[10]	[7]	[8]	[6]	[4]	[3]
3	[10]	[1]	[0]	[3]	[2]	[6]	[11]	[8]	[9]	[7]	[5]	[4]
4	[7]	[10]	[9]	[0]	[11]	[3]	[8]	[5]	[6]	[4]	[2]	[1]
5	[8]	[11]	[10]	[1]	[0]	[4]	[9]	[6]	[7]	[5]	[3]	[2]
6	[4]	[7]	[6]	[9]	[8]	[0]	[5]	[2]	[3]	[1]	[11]	[10]
7	[11]	[2]	[1]	[4]	[3]	[7]	[0]	[9]	[10]	[8]	[6]	[5]
8	[2]	[5]	[4]	[7]	[6]	[10]	[3]	[0]	[1]	[11]	[9]	[8]
9	[1]	[4]	[3]	[6]	[5]	[9]	[2]	[11]	[0]	[10]	[8]	[7]
10	[3]	[6]	[5]	[8]	[7]	[11]	[4]	[1]	[2]	[0]	[10]	[9]
11	[5]	[8]	[7]	[10]	[9]	[1]	[6]	[3]	[4]	[2]	[0]	[11]
12	[6]	[9]	[8]	[11]	[10]	[2]	[7]	[4]	[5]	[3]	[1]	[0]

In order to convert this to a chart of note classes, it is helpful to draw the modular clock, additionally labeling each position by the note class which has the given interval from E, as follows:

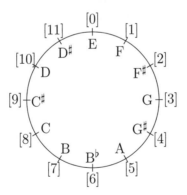

Using this we can translate back to the chart in Chapter 5.

Creating an n-Tone Row Chart Using Modular Arithmetic. This method is equally valid, of course, if we were to create, for some $n \in \mathbb{Z}^+$, an n-tone row chart from an n-tone original row. Given an original row

$$a_1 = [0], a_2, \ldots, a_n$$

from $\mathbb{Z}_n$, we form the $n \times n$ row chart by taking:

$$\boxed{\text{entry } (i, j) = a_j - a_i} \tag{7.4}$$

Here the arithmetic takes place in $\mathbb{Z}_n$.

Example. We will prepare to make a seven-tone composition using this row from $\mathbb{Z}_7$:

$$a_1 = [0] \quad a_2 = [4] \quad a_3 = [1] \quad a_3 = [6] \quad a_4 = [5] \quad a_6 = [2] \quad a_7 = [3] \tag{7.5}$$

We begin by detuning the synthesizer to play in seven-tone equal temperament. Suppose we decide to use the white keys on the keyboard, detuned around C. The 7-chromatic interval is given in cents by $1200/7 \approx 171.43$. Using the method described in Chapter 5, we detune the white keys as follows:

$$
\begin{array}{ccccccc}
\text{C} & \text{D} & \text{E} & \text{F} & \text{G} & \text{A} & \text{B} \\
0 & -29 & -57 & 14 & -14 & -43 & -71
\end{array}
\tag{7.6}
$$

We now associate each of these seven redefined note classes to an element of $\mathbb{Z}_7$ according to its modular interval from C. The following modular clock allows us to easily convert from one to the other.

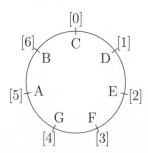

Referring to (7.4), we fill in the rows of the 7×7 row chart with elements of $\mathbb{Z}_7$ using (7.5). This gives the chart below on the left, which translates to the chart on the right using the clock above.

	1	2	3	4	5	6	7
1	[0]	[4]	[1]	[6]	[5]	[2]	[3]
2	[3]	[0]	[4]	[2]	[1]	[5]	[6]
3	[6]	[3]	[0]	[5]	[4]	[1]	[2]
4	[1]	[5]	[2]	[0]	[6]	[3]	[4]
5	[2]	[6]	[3]	[1]	[0]	[4]	[5]
6	[5]	[2]	[6]	[4]	[3]	[0]	[1]
7	[4]	[1]	[5]	[3]	[2]	[6]	[0]

row chart with modular integers

	1	2	3	4	5	6	7
1	C	G	D	B	A	E	F
2	F	C	G	E	D	A	B
3	B	F	C	A	G	D	E
4	D	A	E	C	B	F	G
5	E	B	F	D	C	G	A
6	A	E	B	G	F	C	D
7	G	D	A	F	E	B	C

row chart with note classes

A seven-tone composition based on this row chart might contain the following:

This employs the inversion of the original row, which is the left column of the row chart. The sequence is used three times, first melodically, then twice with some harmonic content. The passage should be played with the detuning given in (7.6).

Exponential Notation in a Group. Let $(G, \cdot)$ be a group, and let $x \in G, n \in \mathbb{Z}^+$. We define x^n to be the n-fold composition $x \cdot x \cdots x$ in G. We define x^0 to be e, the identity element of G. Finally we define x^{-n} to be the n-fold composition $x^{1-} \cdot x^{-1} \cdots x^{-1}$. We have now defined x^n for <u>any</u> $n \in \mathbb{Z}$. With these definitions, the following familiar-looking rules of exponents are valid for any $x \in G$, $n, m \in \mathbb{Z}$:

$$x^{n+m} = x^n \cdot x^m,$$
$$(x^n)^m = x^{nm}. \tag{7.7}$$

We leave it as an exercise to verify these rules.

In the case where the group is commutative and the group law is denoted by $+$, we usually denote the n-fold sum $x + x + \cdots + x$ by nx rather than

x^n. In this situation the rules (7.7) become:

$$(n + m)x = nx + mx \,,$$
$$m(nx) = (nm)x \,. \tag{7.8}$$

Generators and Cyclic Groups. Given $t \in G$, G a group, we call t a *generator* for G if every element of G can be written in the form t^n for some $n \in \mathbb{Z}$; in other words,

$$\{t^n \,|\, n \in \mathbb{Z}\} = G \,.$$

If G has a generator, we call G a *cyclic* group.

Suppose G is cyclic and $t \in G$ is a generator. Consider the set

$$S = \{n \in \mathbb{Z}^+ \,|\, t^n = e\} \,.$$

If $S = \emptyset$, then any two powers t^n and t^m of t will be distinct unless $n = m$, and therefore the elements of G are in one-to-one correspondence with elements of $\mathbb{Z}$, and this correspondence defines an isomorphism of G with $\mathbb{Z}$. This assertion will appear as an exercise.

If $S \neq \emptyset$, then S has a smallest element m, by the Well-Ordering Principle. The positive integer m will be called the *order* of t. We claim that any element $x \in G$ has a unique expression $x = t^r$ with $0 \leq r < m$. This follows from the Division Algorithm: Writing $n = qm + r$ as in the algorithm, we have $t^n = t^{mq+r} = t^{mq} \cdot t^r = (t^m)^q \cdot t^r = e^q \cdot t^r = e \cdot t^r = t^r$. This uses the rules of exponents in (7.7). The uniqueness of r is fairly apparent. If there two integers r and r', with $0 \leq r < r' < m$ and $t^{r'} = t^r$, then we would have $t^{r'-r} = e$ and $r' - r < m$, violating the minimality of m. So the claim is proved, and we see that

$$G = \{e, t, t^2, \ldots, t^{m-1}\}$$

with these elements distinct. Therefore G has precisely m elements.

Example. The group $\mathbb{Z}_m$ is a cyclic group, and $[1]$ is a generator having order m. This is because m is the smallest integer n such that $n[1] = [0]$.

A cyclic group can have more than one generator (and usually does). Consider as an example a group G having a generator t of order 8. In this case G consists of the eight elements

$$e, t, t^2, t^3, t^4, t^5, t^6, t^7 \,.$$

Consider $u = t^3 \in G$. We claim that u is also a generator. We show this directly by writing the powers of u as powers of t. We have $u^2 = (t^3)^2 = t^6$ and $u^3 = (t^3)^3 = t^9 = t$. Continuing in this fashion we get

$$e, \quad u = t^3, \quad u^2 = t, \quad u^4 = t^4, \quad u^5 = t^7, \quad u^6 = t^2, \quad u^7 = t^5$$

and this accounts for all the elements of G.

In Chapter 8 we will see that if t is a generator having order m, then a power t^n is also a generator precisely when the only positive integer dividing both m and n in $\mathbb{Z}$ is 1, i.e., $\gcd(n, m) = 1$.

Generating Intervals. The group of modular n-chromatic intervals is identified with $\mathbb{Z}_n$. We call such an interval a *generating interval* if it generates the group $\mathbb{Z}_n$. These will be the intervals whose iterations give all the n-chromatic intervals.

By the criterion advertised above, these coincide with those classes $[m] \in \mathbb{Z}_n$ for which 1 is the only positive integer dividing m and n. Hence there are $\phi(n)$ generators in $\mathbb{Z}_n$, ϕ being the Euler phi function. With this criterion one easily checks that the generating 12-chromatic intervals are the semitone ([1]), the fourth ([5]), the fifth ([7]), and the major seventh ([11]).

Exercises

1. Which of the following sets, together with the given operation, form a monoid, and of those which are also a group? Justify your answers.

   (a) $\mathbb{Q}$, $+$ (b) $\mathbb{Z}^+$, $\cdot$ (c) $\{-1, 0, 1\}$, $\cdot$

   (d) the set of keyboard intervals, composition of intervals

2. Show that the functions $f(x) = b^x$ and $g(x) = \log_b(x)$ are group homomorphisms, and that they are inverse to each other, thereby giving isomorphisms between the groups $(\mathbb{R}, +)$ and $(\mathbb{R}^+, \cdot)$. Explain how this relates to the measurement of musical intervals.

3. Express the following compositions of modular 12-chromatic intervals as r semitones with $0 \leq r < 12$. Interpret all these compositions as operations in $\mathbb{Z}_{12}$.

   (a) 14 semitones and 23 semitones

   (b) two fifths and a major third

(c) six fifths

(d) up three minor thirds, down six steps

4. Prove using the Division Algorithm that if I is an interval in the n-chromatic scale, the iteration of I n times is equivalent modulo octave to the unison interval. Restate this as an assertion about elements of the group $\mathbb{Z}_n$.

5. Prove that $\mathbb{Z}_n$ has exactly n elements by showing that $[0], [1], \ldots, [n-1]$ are distinct, and that these are all of the elements of $\mathbb{Z}_n$.

6. For each of these choices of n, determine $\phi(n)$ by listing all the generating intervals in the n-chromatic scale. Indicate which pairs of generating intervals are inverse to each other, and for each pair draw the circle of intervals which is based on one element of the pair in the clockwise direction, the other element of the pair in the counter-clockwise direction.

   (a) $n=6$ (b) $n=5$ (c) $n=9$ (d) $n=10$

7. Suppose G is a group and $g \in G$. Show that there is a <u>unique</u> group homomorphism $\varphi : \mathbb{Z} \to G$ such that $\varphi(1) = g$.

8. List all generators for these cyclic groups:

   (a) $(\mathbb{Z}, +)$ (b) $(\{1, -1\}, \cdot)$ (c) $(\mathbb{Z}_7, +)$ (d) $(\mathbb{Z}_{12}, +)$

9. Explain why $(\mathbb{R}, +)$ is not a cyclic group.

10. Create n-tone row charts for the following choices of n and the given sequences of original rows in $\mathbb{Z}_n$:

    (a) $n = 3$; $([2], [0], [1])$

    (b) $n = 5$; $([4], [0], [2], [3], [1])$

    (c) $n = 6$; $([5], [2], [4], [1], [3], [0])$

    (d) $n = 7$; $([3], [5], [6], [0], [2], [1], [4])$

Chapter 8

Algebraic Properties of the Integers

We have identified a musical interval I with a positive real number $x \in \mathbb{R}^+$. Since $\mathbb{Z}^+ \subset \mathbb{R}^+$, each positive integer gives an interval. For example, we have seen that the integer 2 represents the octave, and that the integer 3 is an interval about 2 cents greater than the keyboard's octave-and-a-fifth (1900 cents), as shown by the calculation $1200 \log_2 3 \approx 1901.96$.

$2 = $ octave interval $3 \approx $ octave-and-a-fifth interval $4 = $ two octave interval

We will now investigate some properties of the integers $\mathbb{Z}$ which relate to musical phenomena.

Ring. A non-empty set R endowed with two associative laws of composition $+$ and $\cdot$ is called a *ring* if $(R, +)$ is a commutative group, $(R, \cdot)$ is a monoid, and for any $a, b, c \in R$ we have $a \cdot (b + c) = a \cdot b + a \cdot c$ and $(b + c) \cdot a = b \cdot a + c \cdot a$ (the latter property is called *distributivity*). We call the $+$ operation *addition* and the $\cdot$ operation *multiplication*, and we often denote the latter by dropping the $\cdot$ and simply writing ab for $a \cdot b$. We write 0 and 1 for the additive and multiplicative identity elements, respectively. We say the ring R is *commutative* if the monoid $(R, \cdot)$ is commutative. (We have already insisted that $(R, +)$ is commutative.) We will be dealing only with commutative rings here, so henceforth when we say "ring" we will mean "commutative ring".

Two properties that we would expect to hold for any x in a ring R are these: $(-1) \cdot x = -x$ and $0 \cdot x = 0$. We leave it as an exercise that these properties can indeed be deduced from our assumptions.

Units. We have assumed that $(R, \cdot)$ is a monoid; it will not be a group in general[1] since 0 has no multiplicative inverse. However, some elements of R (1, for example) will have multiplicative inverses. If $x \in R$ is such an element, we call x a *unit,* and we denote its multiplicative inverse[2] by x^{-1}. The set of units in R, sometimes denoted R^*, forms a group with respect to multiplication.

Cancellation. A ring R is called an *integral domain* if whenever $a, b \in R$ with $ab = 0$, then $a = 0$ or $b = 0$.

PROPOSITION (CANCELLATION). *If R is an integral domain, and $a, b, c \in R$ with $a \neq 0$ and $ab = ac$, then $b = c$.*

Proof. We have $0 = ab - ac = a(b - c)$. Since $a \neq 0$ and R is an integral domain, we must have $b - c = 0$, i.e., $b = c$.   □

Examples. The reader should verify the details in the following four examples.

(1) **Integers.** The set of integers $\mathbb{Z}$, taking $+$ and $\cdot$ to be the usual addition and multiplication, is the most basic example of a ring. It is commutative, and it is an integral domain. The group of units is $\mathbb{Z}^* = \{1, -1\}$.

(2) **Real Numbers.** The set $\mathbb{R}$ also becomes a ring under the usual $+$ and $\cdot$. It is also an integral domain. Here we have $\mathbb{R}^* = \mathbb{R} - \{0\}$.

(3) **Rational Numbers.** $\mathbb{Q}$ is an integral domain, sharing with $\mathbb{R}$ the property that all non-zero elements are units.

(4) **Modular Integers.** For $m \in \mathbb{Z}^+$, we give $\mathbb{Z}_m$ a ring structure as follows: The additive group $(\mathbb{Z}_m, +)$ is as before. For $[k], [\ell] \in \mathbb{Z}_m$, define $[k] \cdot [\ell] = [k\ell]$. The proofs that this is well defined and that the axioms for a ring are satisfied by $+$ and $\cdot$ are left as an exercise. Note

---

[1]The only situation when $(R, \cdot)$ is a group is when $R = \{0\}$, which coincides with the case $0 = 1$. In this case R is called the *trivial ring.*

[2]The multiplicative inverse x^{-1} is unique to x. The proof of this mimics the proof that inverses in a group are unique.

that [0] and [1] are the additive and multiplicative identity elements, respectively, of $\mathbb{Z}_m$.

Ideals. A subset $J \subseteq R$ is called an *ideal* if it is a subgroup of the additive group $(R, +)$ and if whenever $a \in R$ and $d \in J$, then $ad \in J$.

One example of an ideal in R is the *zero ideal* $\{0\}$. Any other ideal will be called a *non-zero ideal*. The ring R itself is an ideal.

Given $a \in R$ we can form the set of all multiples of a in R, namely the set

$$aR = \{x \in R \mid x = ab \text{ for some } b \in R\}.$$

Such an ideal is called a *principal ideal*, and the element a is called a generator for the ideal. Note that $\{0\}$ and R are principal ideals by virtue of $\{0\} = 0R$ and $R = 1R$.

If R is an integral domain in which every ideal is principal, we call R a *principal ideal domain,* abbreviated PID.

For example, the set of even integers forms an ideal in $\mathbb{Z}$. This ideal is a principal ideal, since it is equal to $2\mathbb{Z}$. We will now show that:

THEOREM. $\mathbb{Z}$ *is a principal ideal domain.*

Proof. This is based on the Division Algorithm. Let J be an ideal in $\mathbb{Z}$. If $J = \{0\}$, then $J = 0\mathbb{Z}$ and we are done. Otherwise J contains non-zero integers, and since $n \in J$ implies $(-1)n = -n$ is in J, then J must contain some positive integers. Let n be the smallest positive integer in J (such an n exists by the Well-Ordering Principle). We claim that $J = n\mathbb{Z}$. Clearly $n\mathbb{Z} \subseteq J$. To see the other containment, let $m \in J$, and use the Division Algorithm to write $m = qn + r$ with $0 \leq r < n$. Then r is in J since $r = m - qn$. By the minimality of n, we conclude $r = 0$, hence $n = qn \in b\mathbb{Z}$ as desired. $\square$

If $J \subseteq \mathbb{Z}$ is an ideal with $J \neq 0$, and if n is a generator for J, then the only other generator for J is $-n$. This follows easily from the fact that any two generators are multiples of each other, and will be left as an exercise. Thus any non-zero ideal has a unique positive generator.

Greatest Common Divisor. Suppose we are given $m, n \in \mathbb{Z}$, not both zero. The subset $m\mathbb{Z} + n\mathbb{Z}$, by which we mean the set of all integers a which can be written $a = hm + kn$ for some $h, k \in \mathbb{Z}$, is an ideal in $\mathbb{Z}$. Therefore it has a unique positive generator d, which divides both m and n. If e is any other positive integer which divides both m and n, then $m, n \in e\mathbb{Z}$

so $m\mathbb{Z} + n\mathbb{Z} = d\mathbb{Z} \subseteq e\mathbb{Z}$, and hence e divides d. Therefore $d \geq e$ and we (appropriately) call d the *greatest common divisor* of m and n. The greatest common divisor is denoted $\gcd(m, n)$. Since $d\mathbb{Z} = m\mathbb{Z} + n\mathbb{Z}$, there exist integers h, k such that $d = hm + kn$.

To say that $\gcd(m, n) = 1$ is to say that the only common divisors of m and n in $\mathbb{Z}$ are ± 1. In this case we say that m and n are *relatively prime*.

Prime Numbers. A positive integer p is called *prime* if it is divisible in $\mathbb{Z}$ by precisely two positive integers, namely 1 and p. (Note that 1 is not prime by virtue of the word "precisely".) The first ten prime numbers are:

$$2, 3, 5, 7, 11, 13, 17, 19, 23, 29. \tag{8.1}$$

It will be left as an exercise to show that if p is prime and $n \in \mathbb{Z}$, then either p divides n or $\gcd(p, n) = 1$.

Sieve of Eratosthenes. A systematic procedure for finding the prime numbers was given by the Greek astronomer and mathematician Eratosthenes of Cyrene (3rd century BC). We conceive of the positive integers as an infinite list $1, 2, 3, 4, 5, 6, \ldots$, then proceed to cross out certain numbers on the list, as follows. After crossing out 1, we cross out all numbers following 2 which are divisible by 2.

$$\cancel{1}, 2, 3, \cancel{4}, 5, \cancel{6}, 7, \cancel{8}, 9, \cancel{10}, 11, \cancel{12}, 13, \cancel{14}, 15,$$
$$\cancel{16}, 17, \cancel{18}, 19, \cancel{20}, 21, \cancel{22}, 23, \cancel{24}, 25, \cancel{26}, 27, \cancel{28}, 29, \cancel{30}, \ldots.$$

Then we find the next number after 2 which is still on the list, which is 3. We then cross out all numbers following 3 which are not divisible by 3.

$$\cancel{1}, 2, 3, \cancel{4}, 5, \cancel{6}, 7, \cancel{8}, \cancel{9}, \cancel{10}, 11, \cancel{12}, 13, \cancel{14}, \cancel{15},$$
$$\cancel{16}, 17, \cancel{18}, 19, \cancel{20}, \cancel{21}, \cancel{22}, 23, \cancel{24}, 25, \cancel{26}, \cancel{27}, \cancel{28}, 29, \cancel{30}, \ldots.$$

When this process is continued up to an integer n, then the numbers below n which remain on the list are precisely the primes which are $\leq n$.

$$\cancel{1}, 2, 3, \cancel{4}, 5, \cancel{6}, 7, \cancel{8}, \cancel{9}, \cancel{10}, 11, \cancel{12}, 13, \cancel{14}, \cancel{15},$$
$$\cancel{16}, 17, \cancel{18}, 19, \cancel{20}, \cancel{21}, \cancel{22}, 23, \cancel{24}, \cancel{25}, \cancel{26}, \cancel{27}, \cancel{28}, 29, \cancel{30}, \ldots.$$

We have shown that the primes ≤ 30 are the ten integers in the list (8.1) above.

If the procedure were continued infinitely to completion, the complete list of primes would remain.

THEOREM. *If p is a prime number and if p divides mn, where $m, n \in \mathbb{Z}$, then p divides m or p divides n.*

Proof. Suppose p does not divide m. Then $\gcd(m, p) = 1$ and we can write $1 = hm + kp$ for some integers h and k. Multiplying this equation by n gives $n = hmn + kpn$. Note that p divides both summands on the right, since p divides nm. Therefore p divides n. This concludes the proof.   □

One can easily conclude that if a prime number p divides a product $m_1 m_2 \cdots m_s$, then p divides at least one of $m_1, m_2, \ldots, m_s$.

Unique Factorization. We now establish the fact that every positive integer can be factored uniquely as the product of primes.

THEOREM. *Let $n \geq 1$ be an integer. Then n can be factored as*

$$n = p_1^{\alpha_1} p_2^{\alpha_2} \cdots p_r^{\alpha_r}$$

where $r \geq 0$, $p_1, p_2, \ldots, p_r$ are distinct primes, and $\alpha_1, \alpha_2, \ldots, \alpha_r \geq 1$. Moreover, this factorization is unique, meaning that if $n = q_1^{\beta_1} q_2^{\beta_2} \cdots q_t^{\beta_t}$ is another such factorization, then $t = r$ and after rearranging we have $p_1 = q_1$, $p_2 = q_2$, $\ldots$, $p_r = q_r$.

Proof. We first establish the existence of a prime factorization for all integers ≥ 1. If not all positive integers admit a prime factorization, then by the Well-Ordering Principle we can choose a smallest integer n which fails to admit a factorization. We note that n itself could not be prime, otherwise it admits the factorization in the theorem with $r = 1$ and $p_1 = n$. Since n is not prime, it has a positive divisor m which is neither n nor 1. We have $n = m\ell$ and clearly ℓ is neither n nor 1. We must have $1 < m, \ell < n$, so by the minimality of n, both m and ℓ have prime factorizations. But if m and ℓ have prime factorizations, then so does n since $n = m\ell$. This is a contradiction. Hence all integers ≥ 1 have a prime factorization.

It remains to show the uniqueness. If $p_1^{\alpha_1} p_2^{\alpha_2} \cdots p_r^{\alpha_r} = q_1^{\beta_1} q_2^{\beta_2} \cdots q_t^{\beta_t}$, then p_1 divides $q_1^{\beta_1} q_2^{\beta_2} \cdots q_t^{\beta_t}$. Since p_1 is prime it must divide one of $q_1, q_2, \ldots, q_t$. Say p_1 divides q_1. Since q_1 is also prime we must have $p_1 = q_1$, so we can cancel to get $p_1^{\alpha_1 - 1} p_2^{\alpha_2} \cdots p_r^{\alpha_r} = p_1^{\beta_1 - 1} q_2^{\beta_2} \cdots q_t^{\beta_t}$. We continue cancelling p_1 to deduce that $\alpha_1 = \beta_1$. The remaining equation is $p_2^{\alpha_2} \cdots p_r^{\alpha_r} = q_2^{\beta_2} \cdots q_t^{\beta_t}$. As above we can argue that $p_2 = q_2$ (after rearranging) and that $\alpha_2 = \beta_2$. We continue to get the desired result.   □

Modular Integers. The algebraic properties we have established for $\mathbb{Z}$ tell us many things about the rings of modular integers $\mathbb{Z}_m$, for $m \in \mathbb{Z}^+$. One such fact concerns the matter of when an element $[n] \in \mathbb{Z}_m$ is a generator of the additive group $(\mathbb{Z}_m, +)$.

THEOREM. *Given $[n] \in \mathbb{Z}_m$, the following three conditions are equivalent.*

(1) $gcd(m, n) = 1$.

(2) $[n]$ *is a generator of the additive group $(\mathbb{Z}_m, +)$.*

(3) $[n]$ *is a unit in the ring $\mathbb{Z}_m$ (i.e., $[n] \in \mathbb{Z}_m^*$).*

Proof. We first consider conditions (2) and (3). If $[n]$ is a generator of $(\mathbb{Z}_m, +)$, then all elements of $\mathbb{Z}_m$ can be written as $k \cdot [n]$, for some $k \in \mathbb{Z}$. (This is the way we write exponentiation in an additive group.) In particular, we have $[1] = k \cdot [n]$. But, by the definition of multiplication in $\mathbb{Z}_m$, $k \cdot [n] = [k] \cdot [n]$. Therefore $[k] \cdot [n] = [1]$, which shows $[n]$ is a unit. Conversely, if $[n] \in \mathbb{Z}_m^*$, with inverse $[k] = [n]^{-1}$, then for any $[\ell] \in \mathbb{Z}_m$ we have $[\ell] = [\ell] \cdot [1] = [\ell] \cdot [k] \cdot [n] = [\ell k] \cdot [n] = \ell k \cdot [n]$, which shows that $[\ell]$ is a multiple ("power") of $[n]$. Hence $[n]$ is a group generator for $(\mathbb{Z}_m, +)$.

The equivalence of (1) with these conditions, the proof of which uses greatest common divisors, is left as an exercise. $\qquad\square$

Euler Phi Function. For any $m \in \mathbb{Z}^+$, we have defined the *Euler phi function* $\phi(m)$ to be the number of positive integers n with $1 \le n < m$ which are relatively prime to m. According to the above theorem, $\phi(m)$ also counts the number of elements in $\mathbb{Z}_m^*$, and the number of group generators for $(\mathbb{Z}_m, +)$. By virtue of the latter, $\phi(m)$ counts the number of generating intervals in the m-chromatic scale.

For example $\phi(12) = 4$, since the numbers $1, 5, 7, 11$ are precisely the positive integers < 12 which are relatively prime to 12. This reflects the fact that the generating intervals in the 12-chromatic scale are the semitone, the fourth, the fifth, and the major seventh.

Patterns of m on n in Music. Composers sometimes create ingenious musical passages by imposing a pattern of m notes or beats against a pattern of n such, where $gcd(m, n) = 1$. This technique exploits (perhaps unknowingly by the composer) the fact that $[m]$ is a generator in $\mathbb{Z}_n$ (and vice versa).

One way this can occur is by cycling m pitches through a repeated rhythmic pattern of n notes. This is exemplified in the main melodic line of the big band song *In the Mood.* Here $m = 3$ and $n = 4$. The song's "hook" lies in the repetition of the rhythmic figure comprising four eighth notes in swing time, shown below.

The melody repeats the sequence of three pitches C_4, $E_4^\flat$, $A_4^\flat$, through the above rhythmic pattern as follows:

Note that both patterns end their cycle on the twelfth eighth notes and not before. The reason for this lies in the previous theorem. Let the top numbers represent the elements of $\mathbb{Z}_4 = \{[1], [2], [3], [4] = [0]\}$. Identifying each of the bottom numbers with the element of $\mathbb{Z}_4$ represented directly above it, we see the effect of adding $[3]$s successively in $\mathbb{Z}_4$. The multiples of $[3]$ (i.e., the elements of $\mathbb{Z}_4$ lying above the 3s) are, respectively, $[3], [2], [1], [4] = [0]$, which exhausts the set $\mathbb{Z}_4$. This is because, since $\gcd(3, 4) = 1$, $[3]$ is a generator of $\mathbb{Z}_4$, so all four of the numbers 1-4 must appear above the *3*s before any of them makes a repeat appearance above a *3*. Each three-note cycle below starts on a different number 1-4, and the two cycles culminate together only at $3 \times 4 = 12$ eighth notes, and not before.

There is symmetry between the two patterns: We could let the bottom numbers represent elements of $\mathbb{Z}_3 = \{[1], [2], [3] = [0]\}$. Then the cycles above are just adding successive $[4]$s in $\mathbb{Z}_3$. Each of the four-note cycles starts on a different number *1-3*, for all the same reasons as above.

The poignant passage below, from George Gershwin's *Rhapsody in Blue*, exhibits the same phenomenon with $m = 3$, $n = 5$, starting in the third measure.

Here the three pitches $D_4^\sharp$, D_4, and $C_4^\sharp$ are cycled against the five-note rhythmic pattern comprising two eighth notes followed by three quarter notes. The 3 on 5 double pattern completes itself after $3 \times 5 = 15$ notes, occupying measures 3-5. The entire pattern is then repeated in measures 6-8 with different harmony.

Another type of m on n pattern occurs when a melodic figure of duration m beats is repeated in a meter which has the listener counting in groups of n beats. An example of this occurs in the vamp section of the 1971 blues-pop song *Ain't No Sunshine*.

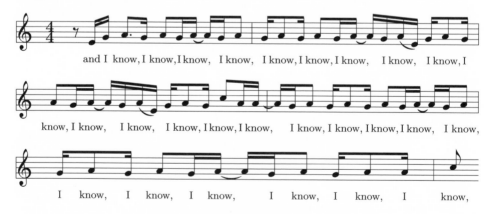

In this example a rhythmic figure comprising a sixteenth note followed by an eighth note (or two tied sixteenth notes) is repeated in $\frac{4}{4}$ time. Since the length of the figure is 3 sixteenth notes, and each measure has 16 sixteenth notes, we view this as a 3 on 16 pattern. Both cycles commence together at the beginning of the second measure, and the double pattern runs its course in three measures, or $3 \times 16 = 48$ sixteenth notes. The m on n pattern represents a form of polyrhythm fundamentally different from the tuplet, here presenting the listener with the choice of counting the beats in groups of m or in groups of n.

Each of these examples is a slightly different "game" played by the composer, and in each the listener gets a sense of fulfillment only when the double pattern is complete.

Exercises

1. Prove that in any (commutative) ring R we have $(-1) \cdot x = -x$ and $0 \cdot x = 0$, for any $x \in R$.

2. Give the prime factorizations of these integers, writing the primes in ascending order, as in $2^3 \cdot 3 \cdot 7^2$.

   (a) 110   (b) 792   (c) 343   (d) 3422   (e) 15×10^{23}

3. Call a musical interval a *prime interval* if its interval ratio is a prime integer; call it a *rational interval* if its interval ratio is a rational number. Show that all rational intervals can be written as compositions of prime intervals and their opposites.

4. Show that the set of prime intervals does not form a monoid under composition of intervals. Show that the set of rational intervals forms a group.

5. To identify all primes $\leq n$, we performed the sieve of Eratosthenes, listing the integers 1 to n, then crossing off 1 and all higher multiples of each m for $1 < m < n$. Actually we could have stopped sooner, just checking m in the interval $1 < m < s$. What s would suffice?

6. Express each of these ideals in $\mathbb{Z}$ in the form $n\mathbb{Z}$, where n is a positive integer:

   (a) $12\mathbb{Z} + 15\mathbb{Z}$ (b) $5\mathbb{Z} + (-20)\mathbb{Z}$

   (c) $10\mathbb{Z} + 44\mathbb{Z}$ (d) $13\mathbb{Z} + 35\mathbb{Z}$

7. Show that the multiplication $[k] \cdot [\ell] = [k\ell]$ in $\mathbb{Z}_n$ is well defined, and that $\mathbb{Z}_n$ is a ring.

8. Verify that $\mathbb{Q}$ (the rational numbers) is a ring, and, in fact, an integral domain. Show that the only ideals in $\mathbb{Q}$ are $\{0\}$ and $\mathbb{Q}$.

9. Prove that there are infinitely many prime numbers. (Hint: If $p_1, \ldots, p_n$ were a complete list of primes, consider a prime factor of $p_1 \cdots p_n + 1$.)

10. Prove that if p is prime and $n \in \mathbb{Z}$, then either $p \mid n$ or $\gcd(p, n) = 1$.

11. Given $m \in \mathbb{Z}^+$ and $n \in \mathbb{Z}$, prove that $[n]$ is a generator for $\mathbb{Z}_m$ if and only if $\gcd(m, n) = 1$. Interpret this as a statement about generating intervals in the modular m-chromatic scale.

12. Prove that m iterations of any m-chromatic interval is a multi-octave, i.e., ℓ octaves for some $\ell \in \mathbb{Z}$. Interpret this as a statement about an element $[k]$ of $\mathbb{Z}_m$, and use this statement to prove that the order r of $[k]$ divides m.

13. Prove that the ring $\mathbb{Z}_n$ is an integral domain precisely when n is a prime number.

14. Compose a brief melodic passage using the m on n technique discussed at the end of this chapter.

Chapter 9

The Integers as Intervals

We will now determine, for each of the first several positive integers $n = 1, 2, 3, \ldots$, which equally tempered scale interval best approximates the interval given by the ratio n and we will calculate the closeness of the approximation. This will tell us how to detune keyboard intervals so that the integer ratios can be heard. Once this is done, it is enlightening to "listen to the integers", noting that each possesses a unique "personality" which seems determined by the integer's prime factorization.

We will occasionally employ the slightly awkward term *integral interval* to refer to a musical interval whose ratio is an integer. We call such an interval a *prime interval* if its ratio is a prime.

The set of integral intervals forms a monoid under composition of intervals; this monoid can be identified with $(\mathbb{Z}, \cdot)$.

One. The ratio 1, representing *unison*, is the identity element of the monoid $(\mathbb{Z}, \cdot)$ of integral intervals, and the identity element of the group $(\mathbb{R}, \cdot)$ of all interval ratios. It is not terribly interesting, since it is the ratio of two frequencies giving the same pitch.

Two. We have noted the fact that the smallest prime, 2, gives the *octave*, which might be called music's most consonant interval. When two notes an octave apart are sounded they blend together almost as one. Octave equivalence is ingrained in musical notation by virtue of the fact that notes which form the interval of one or more octaves are assigned the same letter of the alphabet. Only by using subscripts such as C_2 or $A_5^\flat$ (or by using a musical staff) can we distinguish them notationally.

Moreover, the keyboard's equally tempered chromatic scale is tuned to give a perfect octave (since equal temperament is obtained by dividing the interval given by 2 into 12 equal intervals). Hence the ratio 2 is rendered precisely by equal temperament. The interval from F_2 to F_3, shown below, has frequency ratio exactly 2.

keyboard's exact representation of 2

Three. We have noted that the prime interval 3 is best approximated on the keyboard by 19 semitones, or one octave plus a fifth, shown below as the interval from F_2 to C_4.

keyboard's approximation of 3, $\approx$ 2 cents flat

This approximation is about 2 cents under, since 3 is measured in cents by $1200 \log_2 3 \approx 1901.96$, and 1900 cents is 19 semitones, which is an octave plus a fifth. This is a very good approximation; it is very difficult for most of us to perceive the difference between the octave plus a fifth and the interval given by 3.

Four. The ratio 4 is two octaves by virtue of $4 = 2^2$. It can be played precisely on the keyboard, as can any integer ratio which is a power of two.

keyboard's exact representation of 4

We will see that the powers of 2 are the only positive integers which can be played perfectly on a keyboard tuned to the 12-note equally tempered scale, or in fact on any chromatic scale which equally divides the octave. Yet we will see that harmony derives from the integers.

Five. The next interesting integer ratio is the prime number 5, which is given in cents by $1200 \log_2 5 \approx 2786.31$. The closest interval to this on the keyboard is 2800 cents, which is two octaves plus a major third.

keyboard's approximation of 5, ≈ 14 cents sharp

This is sharp by about 14 cents. Unlike the fifth's approximation of 2, this difference is perceptible, upon a careful listening, by most people with reasonably good pitch discrimination. The tempered scale was shunned for many years primarily because of this particular discrepancy.

Six. The integer $6 = 3 \cdot 2$ is the smallest integer whose prime factorization involves more than one prime. By virtue of the factorization $6 = 2 \cdot 3$, multiplicativity tells us that this interval is obtained by iterating the intervals corresponding to 2 and 3. Thus we get an interval which is approximated on the keyboard by an octave plus an octave plus a fifth, or two octaves and a fifth.

keyboard's approximation of 6, ≈ 2 cents flat

Since the keyboard renders the octave precisely, its rendition of six should have the same error as its approximation of 3, which is about 2 cents. This is verified by the calculation

$$1200 \log_2 6 = 1200(\log_2 2 + \log_2 3)$$
$$= 1200 \log_2 2 + 1200 \log_2 3$$
$$\approx 1200 + 1901.96 = 3101.96$$

which shows the ratio 6 to be about 2 cents greater than 3100 cents $(= 31$ semitones), which is the keyboard's two octaves plus a fifth.

Seven. The prime 7 is the lowest integer which is poorly approximated by the tempered chromatic scale. In cents it is given by $1200 \log_2 7 \approx 3368.83$. The closest interval on the keyboard is 3400 cents, which over-estimates 7's interval by about 31 cents. This approximation is 34 semitones, which equals two octaves plus a minor seventh.

keyboard's approximation of 7, $\approx$ 31 cents sharp

Eight. Continuing, we note that 8, being 2^3, is exactly three octaves, and is rendered precisely on the keyboard.

keyboard's exact representation of 8

Nine. Since $9 = 3^2$, it is approximated by composing the octave-plus-a-fifth interval with itself, which yields two octaves plus a ninth, or three octaves plus a step. This has double the error of the approximation of 3, so the approximation of 9 is about 4 cents flat.

keyboard's approximation of 9, $\approx$ 4 cents flat

Ten. We have $10 = 2 \cdot 5$, hence 10 is approximated by the composition of the octave with the two-octaves-plus-a-third interval, yielding three octaves and a third, and having the same error as the approximation of 5 (since 2 is rendered exactly), which is about 14 cents sharp.

keyboard's approximation of 10, $\approx$ 14 cents sharp

Eleven. The next integer, the prime 11, has the worst tempered scale approximation encountered so far: $1200 \log_2 11 \approx 4151.32$. Notice that it lies very close to halfway between 41 semitones (three octaves plus a fourth) and 42 semitones (three octaves plus a tritone), slightly closer to the latter.

keyboard's approximation of 11, $\approx$ 49 cents sharp

This interval is truly "in the cracks", lying about a quarter step from the closest tempered scale intervals.

Twelve. We note that 12, being $2^2 \cdot 3$, is approximated 14 cents sharp by three octaves plus a fifth.

keyboard's approximation of 12, $\approx$ 2 cents flat

Thirteen. The last integer we will consider here is the prime 13. We have $1200 \log_2 13 \approx 4440.53$, and therefore 13 is best approximated on the keyboard by 44 semitones, or three octaves plus a minor sixth, and the approximation is about 41 cents flat.

keyboard's approximation of 13, $\approx$ 41 cents flat

Summary. The sequence of chromatic notes best approximating the pitch having ratio n with F_2, for $n = 1, 2, 3, \ldots, 13$, is:

The discussion above reveals that some of these approximations are very close, others are not close at all.

Non-Chromatic Nature of Intervals other than Multi-Octaves. Note that the only integral intervals on the keyboard so far are the powers of 2 (multiple octave intervals). The following theorem shows that no other integer ratios n occur on the keyboard.

THEOREM. *The only keyboard intervals which have integer ratios are the powers of* 2.

Proof. Suppose $n \in \mathbb{Z}^+$ is a keyboard interval. This means it is obtained by composing k semitones, for some integer $k \geq 0$. Since the semitone has interval ratio $2^{1/12}$, we have $n = \left(2^{1/12}\right)^k = 2^{k/12}$. Raising this to the power 12, we get $n^{12} = 2^k$. By the unique factorization theorem, n can have only 2 in its prime factorization. $\square$

Exercises

1. For each given note N and integer k: label N by letter and subscript (e.g., $A_4^\flat$); write on the staff the (12-chromatic) note M which best

approximates the pitch having interval ratio k with N; and label M by letter and subscript.

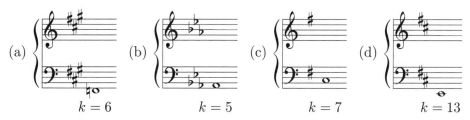

2. For each given pair of positive integers m and n, express in m-chromatic units the m-chromatic scale's best approximation of the integer ratio n, and indicate how many cents sharp or flat the approximation is.

   (a) $m = 7$, $n = 5$

   (b) $m = 19$, $n = 3$

   (c) $m = 13$, $n = 7$

   (d) $m = 4$, $n = 8$

   (e) $m = 23$, $n = 11$

3. List the primes larger than 13 but less than 50, and for each, determine how closely its musical interval is approximated by the keyboard, calculating the error in cents.

4. What chords are closely approximated by these integer ratios (starting from a bottom note that is not in the chord)?

   (a) $2 : 3 : 4 : 5$

   (b) $5 : 6 : 7 : 8$

   (c) $5 : 6 : 7 : 9$

   (d) $10 : 12 : 15 : 18$

5. In the sequence of keyboard approximations of the integer ratios 1 through 13, find all sets of four adjacent notes which can be identified as one of the chords listed in Chapter 3. Look for other chords which appear within the entire sequence.

Chapter 10

Timbre and Periodic Functions

Timbre. The term *timbre* refers to the quality or distinguishing properties of a musical tone <u>other than its pitch</u>, i.e., that which enables one to distinguish between a violin, a trombone, a flute, the vowel ō, or the vowel ē, even though the tones have the same pitch. In order to address this phenomenon we need to discuss a few more concepts relating to functions and graphs.

Piecewise Definitions and Continuity. A function can be defined in piecewise fashion, for example,

$$g(x) = \begin{cases} x, & \text{for } x \leq 1, \\ 1, & \text{for } x > 1, \end{cases}$$

whose graph is:

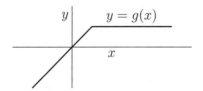

or

$$h(x) = \begin{cases} x, & \text{for } x \leq 1, \\ 2, & \text{for } x > 1, \end{cases}$$

whose graph is:

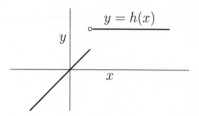

Note the "jump" that appears in the graph of $y = h(x)$ at $x = 1$. This is an example of a *discontinuity*, i.e., the situation at a point $x = a$ at which the function fails to be continuous, as per the following definition.

DEFINITION. *A function $y = f(x)$ is defined to be continuous at $x = a$ if given any $\epsilon > 0$ there exists $\delta > 0$ such that $|f(x) - f(a)| < \epsilon$ whenever $|x - a| < \delta$.*

This says that $f(x)$ will be arbitrarily close to $f(a)$ when x is sufficiently close to a. In the example $h(x)$ above, note that, for $a = 1$ and $\epsilon = 1/2$, there does <u>not</u> exist $\delta > 0$ such that if x lies within δ of 1, then $h(x)$ will lie within $1/2$ of $h(1) = 1$; for as x approaches 1 from above, all values of $h(x)$ are 2.

The function

$$h_1(x) = \begin{cases} x, & \text{for } x < 1, \\ 2, & \text{for } x \geq 1, \end{cases}$$

has the same graph as $h(x)$ except at $x = 1$. We could assign $f(1)$ to be some other number, as in

$$h_2(x) = \begin{cases} x, & \text{for } x < 1, \\ 3, & \text{for } x = 1, \\ 2, & \text{for } x > 1, \end{cases}$$

which has the graph

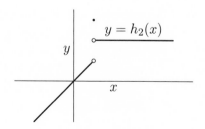

which again has a discontinuity at $x = 1$. It is not hard to prove that there is, in fact, no way to reassign $h(1)$, leaving all other values of h unchanged, in such a way that h is continuous at $x = 1$.

A rough interpretation of a discontinuity is a "jump" in the graph. (This is not precise mathematical terminology, but it serves us pretty well intuitively.) A function which is continuous on an interval I is one whose graph has no "jumps" for any $x \in I$.

Periodic Functions. A function $f(x)$ whose domain is all of $\mathbb{R}$ is called *periodic* if there is a positive number P such that for all $x \in \mathbb{R}$, $f(x + P) = f(x)$. This means that the behavior of the function is completely determined by its behavior on the half-open interval $[0, P)$ (or on any half-open interval of length P).

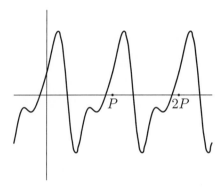

The number P is called the *period* of the function.

Example. The functions $y = \sin x$ and $y = \cos x$ are periodic of period 2π.

Any function $f(x)$ defined on the interval $[0, P)$ can be uniquely extended to a periodic function $g(x)$ of period P whose domain is all of $\mathbb{R}$. This is done by setting $g(x) = f(x - nP)$ for $x \in [nP, (n + 1)P)$ for all integers n. We will refer to this procedure as "extending from $[0, P)$ to $\mathbb{R}$ by periodicity".

Effect of Shifting and Stretching on Periodicity. If $y = f(x)$ is a periodic function with period P, then the vertical and horizontal shifts $y = f(x) + c$ and $y = f(x - c)$ for $c \in \mathbb{R}$ are also periodic of period P, as is the vertical stretch $y = cf(x)$. However the horizontal stretch $y = f(x/c)$ will have period cP. So the effect of stretching horizontally by a factor of c is to divide the frequency of $f(x)$ by c. The proofs of these assertions will be left as an exercise.

Shifting and Stretching Sine and Cosine. The two trigonometric functions $y = \sin x$ and $y = \cos x$ play a central role in the remaining discussion, and they are related as follows: The graph of $y = \cos x$ is obtained by shifting the graph of $y = \sin x$ to the left by $c = \frac{\pi}{2}$. This is because the sine and cosine functions have the relationship

$$\cos x = \sin\left(x + \frac{\pi}{2}\right),$$

which is a special case of the "summation formula"

$$\sin(\alpha + \beta) = \sin\alpha\cos\beta + \cos\alpha\sin\beta. \tag{10.1}$$

Note that the former equation is obtained from the latter by setting $\alpha = x$ and $\beta = \frac{\pi}{2}$, since $\cos\frac{\pi}{2} = 0$ and $\sin\frac{\pi}{2} = 1$.

More generally, if we treat (10.1) as a functional equation by replacing α by the independent variable x and letting β be some fixed number (we might wish to think of β as being an angle measured in radians), we have

$$\sin(x + \beta) = \cos\beta\sin x + \sin\beta\cos x. \tag{10.2}$$

The numbers $\cos\beta$ and $\sin\beta$ are the coordinates of the point Q on the unit circle (i.e., the circle of radius one) centered at the origin, such that the arc length counter-clockwise along the circle from $(1, 0)$ to Q is β.

Let $k, d \in \mathbb{R}$ with $d \geq 0$. Replacing x by kx in (10.2) and multiplying both sides of the above equation by d yields the equation of the function $g(x)$ obtained by starting with $f(x) = \sin x$, shifting to the left by β, compressing horizontally by a factor of k (i.e., stretching by $1/k$), and stretching vertically by a factor of d. The resulting general transformation of $\sin x$ is

$$\boxed{g(x) = d\sin(kx + \beta) = d\left(\cos\beta\sin kx + \sin\beta\cos kx\right).} \tag{10.3}$$

Now let us consider an arbitrary function of the form

$$h(x) = A\sin kx + B\cos kx, \tag{10.4}$$

where $A, B \in \mathbb{R}$ are any numbers. The point (A, B) has distance $\sqrt{A^2 + B^2}$ from the origin. If A and B are not both zero, then letting

$$a = \frac{A}{\sqrt{A^2 + B^2}}, \quad b = \frac{B}{\sqrt{A^2 + B^2}},$$

the point (a, b) has distance 1 from the origin, hence lies on the unit circle centered at the origin. Thus there is an angle β for which $a = \cos \beta, b = \sin \beta$, and letting $d = \sqrt{A^2 + B^2}$ we have

$$h(x) = d \left(a \sin kx + b \cos kx\right)$$
$$= d \left(\cos \beta \sin kx + \sin \beta \cos kx\right)$$
$$= d \sin(kx + \beta).$$

Therefore $h(x)$ is a transformation of $\sin x$ having the form (10.3), where $d = \sqrt{A^2 + B^2}$. The angle β is called the *phase shift*, and the number $d \geq 0$ is the *amplitude*.

Example. Consider the function $h(x) = 3 \sin x + 2 \cos x$. We have $A = 3$, $B = 2$, $d = \sqrt{3^2 + 2^2} = \sqrt{13}$, $a = \frac{3}{\sqrt{13}}$, and $b = \frac{2}{\sqrt{13}}$. The angle β is an acute angle (since the point $(3, 2)$ lies in the first quadrant, so β can be found on a calculator by taking $\arcsin \frac{2}{\sqrt{13}} \approx 0.588$. Thus we have

$$h(x) = \sqrt{13} \left(\frac{3}{\sqrt{13}} \sin x + \frac{2}{\sqrt{13}} \cos x\right)$$
$$= \sqrt{13} \left(\cos \beta \sin x + \sin \beta \cos x\right)$$
$$= \sqrt{13} \sin(x + \beta),$$

where $\beta \approx 0.588$. The amplitude is $\sqrt{13}$ and the phase shift is $\beta \approx 0.588$.

Vibrations. We will use the term *vibration* to mean an oscillation having a pattern which repeats every interval of P units of time. The frequency of the vibration, i.e., the number of repetitions of its pattern per unit of time, is $1/P$. For our purposes, time will be measured in seconds, thereby giving frequency in hertz (vibrations per second). If we realize a vibration as the up and down motion of a point, the vibration is given by a function $y = f(t)$ where y is the position of the particle at time t. The function will be periodic, the period being the number P above. For the remainder of this section t will be used as the independent variable of periodic functions, to suggest time.

Vibrating motion can arise from the strings of a violin, a column of air inside a trumpet, or the human vocal cords. The vibration is transmitted through the air by contraction and expansion (this is called a sound wave) and received by the human ear when the ear drum is set in motion, vibrating in the same pattern as the vibrating object. The brain interprets the vibration as a musical tone. If the vibration has period P, measured in seconds, then the pitch, or frequency, of the tone will be $F = 1/P$ Hz.

Musical Tones and Periodic Functions. Given any periodic function $y = f(t)$ of period P, we can contemplate an oscillating object whose position at time t is $f(t)$ and ask what is the sound of such a vibration. We would expect the pitch of the tone to be $1/P$ Hz, but we wish to investigate what other aspects of $y = f(t)$ determine the character, or timbre, of the sound we are hearing.

If a function $y = f(t)$ did in fact represent the position of an object, we would expect the function $f(t)$ to be continuous. This is based on the supposition that the object's position does not "jump" instantly. Although this is indeed a reflection of reality, our discussion will nevertheless associate a vibration with any periodic function $y = f(t)$ of period $P \in \mathbb{R}^+$ satisfying the following more general properties:

1. f has only finitely many discontinuities on $[0, P)$.

2. f is *bounded*, i.e., there are numbers $b, B \in \mathbb{R}$ such that for all $t \in \mathbb{R}$, $b < f(t) < B$.

We interpret the discontinuities as moments at which the vibrating object's position changes very quickly, so that the transition from one location to another seems instantaneous. This exemplifies the fact that mathematics presents models of physical phenomena, not exact representations.

Suppose $y = f(t)$ is a periodic function, with period P, satisfying the above two conditions. As described above, $f(t)$ is associated to a tone of pitch (frequency) $F = 1/P$. According to our observations about the effect of shifting on periodicity, the pitch is not changed if we alter $f(t)$ by a horizontal shift. Since such a shift can be thought of as a delay, we would not expect it to affect the timbre of the tone, and in fact it does not. The vertical shift describes a motion with altered amplitude, but with the same pitch and the same basic "personality". Observation confirms that such a stretch adjusts the loudness, with very little effect, if any, on the timbre of the tone. The horizontal compression $y = f(ct)$ changes the period to P/c, hence the pitch to $1/(P/c) = c/P = cF$. So the effect of compressing horizontally by a factor of c is to multiply the frequency of $f(t)$ by c.

Effect of Horizontal Stretching on Pitch. The final observation above tells us how to apply a horizontal compression to $f(t)$ to achieve any desired pitch (frequency) r. Suppose the period P is given in seconds. We want $r = cF = \frac{c}{P}$, which gives $c = rP$. Thus the function

$$y = f(rPt)$$

represents a tone having frequency r cycles per second, i.e., r Hz.

Example. Suppose $y = \sin t$ gives motion in seconds. Here $P = 2\pi$, so the frequency is $1/2\pi$ Hz (which is way below the threshold of human audibility). Let us adjust the pitch to give A_4, tuned to $r = 440$ Hz. Accordingly we write $y = \sin(rPt)$, i.e.,

$$y = \sin(880\pi t).$$

The tone given by a sine function as above is sometimes called a "pure tone". It is a non-descript hum, very similar to the tone produced by a tuning fork.

Fourier Theory. We will describe how all periodic functions having reasonably good behavior can be written in terms of the functions $\sin t$ and $\cos t$. This is a fundamental result of harmonic analysis, more specifically Fourier theory, which is based on work of the French mathematician and physicist Joseph Fourier (1768-1830). We first make the following observations.

The first is that if $f(t)$ and $g(t)$ are two functions which are periodic of period P, then so is $(f + g)(t)$, which is defined as $f(t) + g(t)$. This is elementary: $(f + g)(t + P) = f(t + P) + g(t + P) = f(t) + g(t) = (f + g)(t)$. More generally, one sees that if $f_1(t), \ldots, f_n(t)$ are periodic of period P, then so is $\sum_{k=1}^{n} f_k(t)$.

Secondly, suppose $f(t)$ is periodic of period P, and $k \in \mathbb{Z}^+$. As we have seen, the function $f(kt)$ has as its graph the graph of $f(t)$ compressed horizontally by a compression factor of k, and it has period P/k. However, it also has period P, since $f(k(t + P)) = f(kt + kP) = f(kt)$. Obviously the function $af(kt)$, for any $a \in \mathbb{R}$, is also periodic of period P. Therefore a sum $\sum_{k=1}^{n} a_k f(kt)$, where $a_1, \ldots, a_n \in \mathbb{R}$, is again periodic of period P. In particular, a sum $\sum_{k=1}^{n} a_k \sin(kt)$ has period 2π.

The following theorem, basic to harmonic analysis, entails two concepts from calculus which go well beyond the scope of this course: the derivative and the infinite summation.

THEOREM. *Suppose $f(t)$ is periodic of period 2π which is bounded and has a bounded continuous derivative at all but finitely many points in $[0, 2\pi)$. Then there is a real number C and sequences of real numbers $A_1, A_2, A_3, \ldots$ and $B_1, B_2, B_3, \ldots$ such that, for all t at which $f(t)$ is continuous we have $f(t)$ represented by the convergent sum*

$$f(t) = C + \sum_{k=1}^{\infty} [A_k \sin(kt) + B_k \cos(kt)]. \tag{10.5}$$

Note that there is a condition on $f(t)$ beyond the conditions 1 and 2 stated earlier in this chapter. It involves the concept of derivative, which one learns in calculus. The condition roughly says that, away from finitely many points, the graph of $f(t)$ is smooth and that it doesn't slope up or down too much.

The real numbers whose existence is asserted in the above theorem are called *Fourier coefficients*. The infinite summation (10.5), called the *Fourier series* for f, is based on the notions of limit and convergence, also from calculus. With the proper definitions and development, it becomes possible for an infinite sum to have a limit, i.e., to "add up" (converge) to a number. An example is the sum $\sum_{k=0}^{\infty} \frac{1}{2^k} = 1 + \frac{1}{2} + \frac{1}{4} + \frac{1}{8} + \cdots$, which has 2 as its limit. This is the same sum as formula (2.2) from Chapter 2, encountered in our discussion of dotted notes.

The moral of the story told in the above theorem is that well-behaved periodic functions can be approximated by a series of multiples of the sine and cosine functions. There is more to the story, which, again, can be understood by anyone familiar with calculus: The coefficients in formula (10.5) are uniquely determined by the integrals below.

$$C = \frac{1}{2\pi} \int_0^{2\pi} f(t) \, dt \,,$$

$$A_k = \frac{1}{\pi} \int_0^{2\pi} \sin(kt) f(t) \, dt \,, \qquad (10.6)$$

$$B_k = \frac{1}{\pi} \int_0^{2\pi} \cos(kt) f(t) \, dt.$$

If $g(t)$ is a function of arbitrary period P, then $g(\frac{P}{2\pi}t)$ has period 2π, hence we have

$$g\left(\frac{P}{2\pi}t\right) = C + \sum_{k=1}^{\infty} [A_k \sin(kt) + B_k \cos(kt)]$$

by the theorem. Recovering $g(t)$ by replacing t by $\frac{2\pi t}{P}$ in the above, we get the Fourier series for an arbitrary function of period P, satisfying the other hypotheses of the theorem:

$$g(t) = C + \sum_{k=1}^{\infty} \left[A_k \sin \frac{2\pi kt}{P} + B_k \cos \frac{2\pi kt}{P} \right]. \qquad (10.7)$$

Harmonics and Overtones. Associating the function $g(t)$ having period P as above with a musical tone of pitch $F = 1/P$, let us note that

$$g(t) = C + \sum_{k=1}^{\infty} [A_k \sin(2\pi F k t) + B_k \cos(2\pi F k t)] .$$

Each summand $A_k \sin(2\pi F k t) + B_k \cos(2\pi F k t)$ in (10.7) has the form (10.4), and therefore represents a transformation of $\sin(2\pi F k t)$ which can be written in the form (10.3) as

$$d_k [\cos \beta_k \sin(2\pi F k t) + \sin \beta_k \cos(2\pi F k t)] = d_k \sin(2\pi F k t + \beta_k) ,$$

where

$$d_k = \sqrt{A_k^2 + B_k^2}, \qquad \cos \beta_k = \frac{A_k}{d_k}, \qquad \sin \beta_k = \frac{B_k}{d_k}$$

(provided A_k and B_k are not both zero). Hence we have

$$g(t) = C + \sum_{k=1}^{\infty} d_k \sin(2\pi F k t + \beta_k) . \tag{10.8}$$

The k-th summand $d_k \sin(2\pi F k t + \beta_k)$ is obtained from $\sin t$ via shifting by β_k (the k-th phase shift), compressing horizontally by a factor of k and stretching vertically by a factor of d_k (the k-th amplitude). This function has the same basic sound (pitch and timbre) as $\sin(2\pi k F t)$, with a volume adjustment resulting from the amplitude d_k. It is called the k-th *harmonic* of the function $g(t)$. For $k \geq 1$ it is also called the $(k - 1)$-st *overtone* of $g(t)$. When isolated, this harmonic gives the pitch kF, so the sequence of pitches associated to the harmonics gives the sequence of integer ratios with the fundamental frequency F. These are the intervals discussed in Chapter 9; recall that if we take F_2 as the fundamental (first harmonic), the first 13 harmonics are approximated on the keyboard as follows:

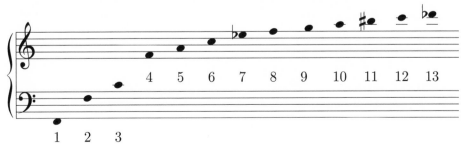

For a given fundamental frequency F, the infinite sequence of pitches

$$F,\ 2F,\ 3F,\ 4F,\ 5F,\ldots$$

is called its *overtone series.*

For a given pitch, it is the relative sizes of the (non-negative) amplitudes $d_1, d_2, d_3, \ldots$ that determine the timbre, or "personality", of a sustained tone, allowing us to distinguish between different musical voices and instruments. We can think of d_k as the "weight" or "degree of presence" of the k-th harmonic in the sound represented by $g(t)$. The timbre of the tone seems to depend on this sequence alone, independent of the sequence of phase shifts $\beta_1, \beta_2, \beta_3, \ldots$, which certainly affect the shape of the graph of $g(t)$, but not the sound.

Overtones (harmonics) are generally not perceived by the ear as pitches; rather the totality of those overtones that fall into audible range are heard as an integrated single tone, with harmonics determining the timbre as explained above. However there are times when overtones <u>can</u> actually be heard as pitches. Overtone singing is a type of singing in which the singer manipulates the resonating cavities in the mouth by moving the tongue and jaw so as to isolate specific overtones one at a time. The isolated overtone then becomes clearly audible. While holding a constant fundamental pitch the singer can thereby "play a tune" with the overtones.

Another situation where overtones can become audible occurs when a certain pitch appears as a *reinforced overtone,* i.e., is an overtone of two or more notes in a well-tuned chord. For example, suppose a chord has root C_3 and fifth G_3. Note, then, that G_4 is the third harmonic of the root[1] and is the second harmonic of the fifth.

G_4, the small note, appears in the overtone series of both C_3 and G_3.

Since G_3 is reinforced, it is sometimes heard as a pitch. Its audibility is even more likely if it lies within a formant (a term to be explained later in the chapter) for the vowel being sung or the instruments playing the

---

[1]Actually it is off by about two cents, as per the discussion in Chapter 9.

chord. Singers of *a cappella* music often say the chord "rings" when this phenomenon is experienced.

Example: The Square Wave. To illustrate the use of the theorem, and equations (10.6), (10.7), and (10.8), to calculate harmonics of a tone, we consider a so-called "square wave", the periodic function defined on the interval $[0, 2\pi)$ by

$$s(t) = \begin{cases} 1, & \text{for } 0 \le t < \pi, \\ -1, & \text{for } \pi \le t < 2\pi, \end{cases}$$

and extended by periodicity to a function whose domain is $\mathbb{R}$. The graph of one period, over $[0, 2\pi)$, appears below.

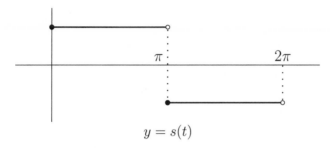

$$y = s(t)$$

This waveform, encountered in electronics and signal processing and available in most synthesizers, produces a distinctive timbre that vaguely resembles the sound of a clarinet. The function satisfies the hypothesis of the theorem, so we wish to use (10.6) to calculate the coefficients C, A_k, and B_k that appear in its Fourier series.

At this point we will fall back on the common interpretation of the integral which asserts that for a well-behaved function $y = f(x)$ the integral $\int_a^b f(x)\, dx$ gives the area enclosed between the graph of $f(x)$ and the x-axis between the vertical lines $x = a$ and $x = b$, with the caveat that area below the axis assumes negative value. Though not mathematically rigorous, this informal realization of the integral will serve here as a working definition, as it will allow the reader who is not familiar with calculus to follow the discussion.

According to (10.6) we have $C = \frac{1}{2\pi} \int_0^{2\pi} s(t)\, dt$. It now becomes apparent from the graph of $s(t)$ that $\int_0^{2\pi} s(t)\, dt = 0$, since the rectangle enclosed above the t-axis between 0 and π has the same area as the one below the axis between π and 2π. Hence $C = 0$.

Now let us consider the coefficients $B_k = \frac{1}{\pi} \int_0^{2\pi} \cos(kt) s(t)\, dt$ (again from (10.6)). First, let's observe that, for $k \in \mathbb{Z}$, the graph of $y = \cos(kt)$ is symmetric around $t = \pi$, in other words $\cos(k(\pi - t)) = \cos(k(\pi + t))$. This can be surmised from the graph, exhibited below for $k = 2$ and $k = 5$,

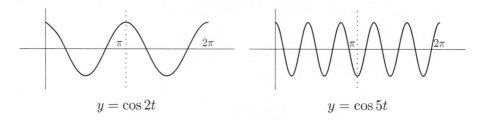

$$y = \cos 2t \qquad\qquad\qquad y = \cos 5t$$

and it follows easily from the summation formula

$$\cos(\alpha + \beta) = \cos\alpha \cos\beta - \sin\alpha \sin\beta \,. \qquad (10.9)$$

(The derivation using this formula will appear as an exercise at the end of this chapter.) Consequently we see that

$$\int_0^\pi \cos(kt)\,dt = \int_\pi^{2\pi} \cos(kt)\,dt \,. \qquad (10.10)$$

Appealing to basic properties of the integral which are apparent from our working definition, and recalling the definition of $s(t)$, we have

$$\begin{aligned}
\int_0^{2\pi} \cos(kt)s(t)\,dt &= \int_0^\pi \cos(kt)s(t)\,dt + \int_\pi^{2\pi} \cos(kt)s(t)\,dt \\
&= \int_0^\pi \cos(kt)\cdot 1\,dt + \int_\pi^{2\pi} \cos(kt)\cdot(-1)\,dt \\
&= \int_0^\pi \cos(kt)\,dt - \int_\pi^{2\pi} \cos(kt)\,dt \\
&= 0\,,
\end{aligned}$$

with the last equality owing to (10.10). This shows $B_k = 0$.

In order to evaluate $A_k = \frac{1}{\pi}\int_0^{2\pi} \sin(kt)s(t)\,dt$, we make some observations about the behavior of $\sin(kt)$ on the interval $[0, 2\pi]$. Specifically, we want to see how its graph on $[0, \pi]$ compares to its graph on $[\pi, 2\pi]$. Now $\sin(kt)$ has period $2\pi/k$, each period being a horizontal compression the graph of $y = \sin t$ over the interval $[0, 2\pi]$, thus comprising an "upper lobe" and a "lower lobe", each enclosing the same amount of area between the graph and the t-axis. From this it follows that the integral of $\sin(kt)$ over any one period, or over any number of complete periods, is zero. Moreover, the point $t = \pi$ lies either at the point between two adjacent periods or at the midpoint of a period, depending on whether k is even or odd, respectively.

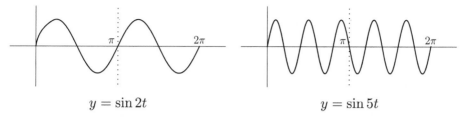

$$y = \sin 2t \qquad\qquad\qquad y = \sin 5t$$

In the case k is even (see $k = 2$ above), the graph looks exactly the same on both intervals, thus the integral over both intervals is the same (and in fact equal to zero, since each period has the same amount of area below the t-axis as above). Therefore $\int_0^{2\pi} \sin(kt)s(t)\, dt = \int_0^\pi \sin(kt)s(t)\, dt + \int_\pi^{2\pi} \sin(kt)s(t)\, dt = \int_0^\pi \sin(kt) \cdot 1\, dt + \int_\pi^{2\pi} \sin(kt) \cdot (-1)\, dt = \int_0^\pi \sin(kt)\, dt - \int_\pi^{2\pi} \sin(kt)\, dt = 0 - 0 = 0$. Hence we have $A_k = 0$ when k is even.

When k is odd (see $k = 5$ above), write $k = 2n + 1$ and note that the interval $[0, \pi]$ contains n complete periods, plus the upper lobe of another; the interval $[\pi, 2\pi]$ has the lower lobe of the $(n + 1)$-st period followed by n complete periods. Since the integral over complete periods is zero we see then that $\int_0^\pi \sin(kt)\, dt = R$ and $\int_\pi^{2\pi} \sin(kt)\, dt = -R$, where R is the area under one upper lobe. Therefore

$$
\begin{aligned}
\int_0^{2\pi} \sin(kt)s(t)\, dt &= \int_0^\pi \sin(kt)s(t)\, dt + \int_\pi^{2\pi} \sin(kt)s(t)\, dt \\
&= \int_0^\pi \sin(kt) \cdot 1\, dt + \int_\pi^{2\pi} \sin(kt) \cdot (-1)\, dt \\
&= \int_0^\pi \sin(kt)\, dt - \int_\pi^{2\pi} \sin(kt)\, dt \\
&= R - (-R) = 2R
\end{aligned}
\tag{10.11}
$$

and we are reduced to evaluating R. We appeal to another intuitive maxim: When a region is stretched horizontally by a factor of a the area of the stretched region equals the area of the original region multiplied by a. Accordingly,

$$R = \frac{1}{k} \int_0^\pi \sin t\, dt \tag{10.12}$$

and here, alas, we appeal to the Fundamental Theorem of Calculus for one brief calculation and ask the general reader's forbearance:

$$\int_0^\pi \sin t\, dt = -\cos t \,\Big|_0^\pi = -\cos \pi + \cos 0 = -(-1) + 1 = 2\,. \tag{10.13}$$

This says the area under one upper lobe of the standard sine (or cosine) curve is 2. Using (10.11), (10.12), and (10.13) we get

$$A_k = \frac{1}{\pi} \int_0^{2\pi} \sin(kt)s(t)\, dt = \frac{1}{\pi} 2R = \frac{4}{k\pi}$$

for k odd.

To summarize, we have shown:

$$C = 0, \qquad B_k = 0 \text{ for all } k, \qquad A_k = \begin{cases} 0, & \text{for } k \text{ even,} \\ \frac{4}{k\pi}, & \text{for } k \text{ odd.} \end{cases}$$

Writing the odd positive integers as $k = 2n+1$ for $n = 0, 1, 2, \ldots$ and pulling the common factor $4/\pi$ to the left, the summation (10.7) for the function $s(t)$ reads:

$$s(t) = \frac{4}{\pi} \sum_{n=0}^{\infty} \frac{1}{2n+1} \sin((2n+1)t) \,. \tag{10.14}$$

Note that the absence of cosines in the series says that the phase shifts β_k are all zero and the amplitudes d_k are 0 for k even, $4/k\pi$ for k odd.

It is interesting (and fun!) to "watch" the summation (10.14) converge by plotting the graph of the truncated series $\frac{4}{\pi} \sum_{n=0}^{N} \frac{1}{2n+1} \sin((2n+1)t)$ for larger and larger N. Note how the graphs below increasingly resemble the graph of $s(t)$.

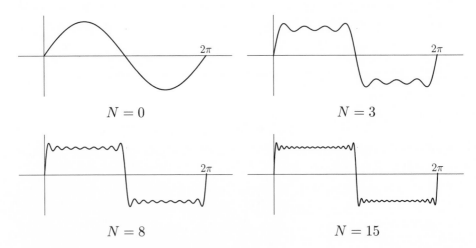

$$N = 0 \qquad\qquad\qquad\qquad N = 3$$

$$N = 8 \qquad\qquad\qquad\qquad N = 15$$

We should remark that all but finitely many overtones lie outside the range of human audibility. Hence some truncation of the Fourier series suffices to represent the audible sound.

For reasons rooted in physics of sound, the clarinet also has only odd harmonics, which explains the faint resemblance of its sound to that of the square wave.

Formants. Suppose a waveform is given by equation (10.8), and suppose we vary only the pitch F, keeping the numbers d_k fixed. (We won't worry about the numbers β_k since they don't contribute much to the character of the sound.) Then the amplitude of each harmonic remains unchanged. This would be the case if we sounded the square wave at different frequencies. The weights of the harmonics are not affected.

However this is not what happens when a musical instrument or a singer changes pitch. Rather, the harmonics that fall within certain frequency ranges will consistently have larger weights than those which do not. These frequency ranges, called *formants,* depend only on the musical instrument being played or the human vowel sound being sung; they remain unchanged as the pitch F varies. Thus each weight d_k will change from note to note, depending on whether the k-th harmonic lies within one of these formants.

This explains why speeding up or slowing down a recording distorts the sound beyond simply changing the pitch. When a recorded tone is played at a different rate from which it was recorded, the sound wave is simply stretched or compressed over time, i.e., the frequency F is changed, with all other parameters in (10.8) remaining unaltered. Thus the formants are not preserved, but rather shifted along with F.[2] Speeding up recorded music produces the familiar "chipmunk effect". Music which is slowed down sounds dark and muddy. In either case the character of the music is changed in a rather comical way.

Musical sounds tend to have two or three formants. These formants are created by the resonating chambers inside the instrument or mouth of the singer. A chamber favors a certain frequency range, determined by its size and shape; frequencies within that range are amplified.

As examples, we will consider the three vowel sounds as typically spoken by Americans. The vowel *oo* (as in "food") has three formants centered respectively near 310 Hz, 870 Hz, and 2250 Hz. The vowel *ah* (as in "father") has formants around 710 Hz, 1100 Hz, and 2640 Hz. The vowel *ee* (as in "feed") has formants at 280 Hz, 2250 Hz, and 2900 Hz. The graphs which plot loudness (vertical axis) against pitch (in Hz) for these vowels look something like the following.

---

[2]Modern studio editing now allows recorded tones to be transposed (i.e., pitch altered) in a way that keeps the formants intact, thus preserving the character of the sound. This process is highly sophisticated and represents a great triumph in signal analysis technology.

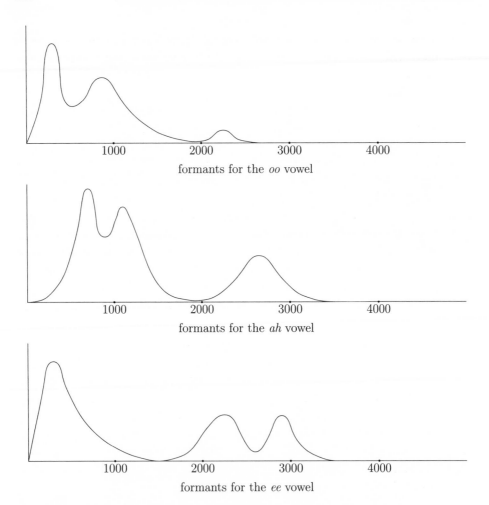

formants for the *oo* vowel

formants for the *ah* vowel

formants for the *ee* vowel

We often use the word "bright" to describe sounds with one or more prominent high formants, and "dark" for sounds whose formants all lie low. Note
that the *ee* vowel has higher second and third upper formants than the other
two, which accounts for its relatively bright sound. Note also that a formant
will have no effect on the timbre if the fundamental pitch being sung lies
above that formant; hence if a soprano sings A_5 (880 Hz) on an *oo* vowel,
the lowest formant, centered around 310 Hz, has no harmonics to amplify.

Musical instruments also possess characterizing formants. For example,
the clarinet has formants in the ranges 1500-1700 Hz, and the trumpet has
a formant in the range 1200-1400 Hz and another centered narrowly around
2500 Hz.

Finally we should acknowledge that the term "loudness" used above is
subjective and difficult to quantify, as it varies from person to person. It is

not directly proportional to mere amplitude. Physics attempts to measure it as a function of "sound pressure", measured in *decibels,* as well as frequency.

Exercises

1. Prove that if $y = f(t)$ has period P, then so does $y = f(t) + c$, $y = f(t - c)$, and $y = cf(t)$, for any $c \in \mathbb{R}$. Prove that $f(t/c)$ $(c \neq 0)$ has period cP.

2. Show that if a periodic function $f(t)$ has period P, then it also has period nP for any positive integer n. Note that the determination of the Fourier coefficients C, A_k, and B_k depend on the choice of period for $f(t)$ (see equation (10.7)). How do these coefficients for f as a function of period kP compare to those obtained from viewing f as a function of period P?

3. Suppose the function $y = f(t)$ is the periodic function of period P corresponding to a musical tone, and suppose the graph of $y = f(t)$ is:

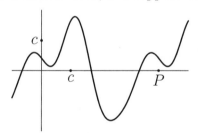

For each of the functions below, sketch its graph and explain how its associated tone compares with that of $f(t)$.

(a) $y = \frac{1}{2}f(t)$ (b) $y = f(2t)$

(c) $y = f(t) + c$ (d) $y = f(t + c)$

4. Find the value α for which the pitch associated to the periodic function $y = \sin(\alpha t)$, where t is time in seconds, is:

     (a) middle C   (b) $A_2^\flat$ (c) $D_6^\sharp$

5. Find the period, frequency, amplitude, and phase shift for these functions, and express each in the form $A\sin(\alpha t) + B\cos(\alpha t)$.

    (a) $f(t) = 5\sin(30\pi t + \frac{\pi}{4})$

    (b) $g(t) = \sqrt{2}\sin(800t + \pi)$

    (c) $h(t) = -\frac{5}{3}\sin(2000t + \arcsin(0.7))$

6. Find the period, frequency, amplitude, and phase shift for these functions, and express each in the form $d\sin(\alpha t + \beta)$:

    (a) $f(t) = 4\sin(300t) + 5\cos(300t)$

    (b) $g(t) = 2\sin(450\pi t) - 2\cos(450\pi t)$

    (c) $h(t) = -\sin(1500\pi t) + 3\cos(1500\pi t)$

7. Suppose musical tone with pitch B_4 has harmonics 1, 3, 5 only, with amplitudes 1, $\frac{1}{9}$, $\frac{1}{25}$, respectively, and phase shifts 0, π, $-\frac{\pi}{2}$, respectively. Suppose also that the vertical shift C is 0. Write its Fourier series in the form $\sum[A_k\sin(kt) + B_k\cos(kt)]$.

8. Verify the formula $\cos(k(\pi - x)) = \cos(k(\pi + x))$ using the formula (10.9). Recall this formula was used in showing the Fourier coefficients B_k for the square wave function are all zero.

9. This is a challenging exercise. Let $q(t)$ be defined by $q(t) = \frac{1}{\pi}t - 1$ on the interval $[0, 2\pi)$, extended to a periodic function on $\mathbb{R}$ by periodicity. This a *sawtooth wave*. Its graph on $[0, 2\pi)$ is:

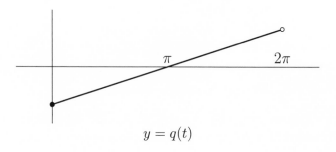

$y = q(t)$

The sound of this waveform is a harsh buzz. Show that

$$q(t) = -\frac{2}{\pi} \sum_{k=1}^{\infty} \frac{1}{k} \sin(kt).$$

(Hint: Mimic the computation for the square wave. You will need the formula

$$\int_0^{2\pi} t \sin(kt)\, dt = -\frac{2\pi}{k},$$

which calculus students should verify using integration by parts.)

10. In the spirit of the last exercise, find the Fourier series for the *triangle wave* given on $[0, 2\pi)$ by

$$r(t) = \begin{cases} \frac{2}{\pi} t - 1, & \text{for } 0 \le t < \pi, \\ -\frac{2}{\pi} t + 3, & \text{for } \pi \le t < 2\pi, \end{cases}$$

which looks like

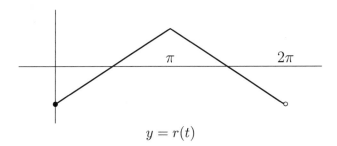

$$y = r(t)$$

You should find that the triangle wave, like the square wave, has only odd harmonics. However the weights of the higher harmonics diminish faster than those of the square wave, hence its sound is less harsh.

11. We saw that the square wave had only odd harmonics. What can you say about the periodicity of a waveform that has only even harmonics? This relates to Exercise 2.

12. The human *ee* vowel has a formant centered at 2900 Hz. What pitch should one sing in order for the fifth harmonic to be maximally amplified by this formant?

13. Two instruments play the pitches A_2 and E_3, making the interval of a keyboard fifth. Suppose they are playing the same kind of instrument,

and that the instrument has a formant centered at 3000 Hz. Suppose the formant amplifies pitches within 400 Hz of its center. Identify the harmonics produced by each instrument which will be amplified by the formant, and give their frequencies. How many pairs of these frequencies are almost aligned? Could this "near alignment" be perfected by slightly adjusting the interval? Might this induce the performers to make such an adjustment, if the instrument permitted?

Chapter 11

The Rational Numbers as Musical Intervals

The rational numbers $\mathbb{Q}$ are a subset of $\mathbb{R}$ containing $\mathbb{Z}$, and we also have the containments $\mathbb{Z}^+ \subset \mathbb{Q}^+ \subset \mathbb{R}^+$. We have noted that elements of $\mathbb{R}^+$ are in one-to-one correspondence with the set of musical intervals, and that this gives a group isomorphism from the group of intervals with $(\mathbb{R}^+, \cdot)$. In the last chapter we examined those intervals which correspond to positive integers, i.e., lie in the monoid $(\mathbb{Z}^+, \cdot)$. Now we will consider those intervals which correspond to elements of the subgroup $(\mathbb{Q}^+, \cdot)$.

It has long been acknowledged that two pitches sounded simultaneously create an effect that we are prone to call "harmonious" or "consonant" when the ratio of their frequencies can be expressed as a ratio $n : m$ where m and n are small positive integers. The smaller the integers, the more consonant the interval. We refer to such intervals as *just* intervals.

Rational Intervals. To say that an interval I is given by a ratio $n : m$ of positive integers is to say that it corresponds to a positive rational number.

DEFINITION. *An interval I will be called rational if its corresponding ratio lies in $\mathbb{Q}^+$. Otherwise we say I is an irrational interval.*

In ancient times such intervals could be accurately created with a vibrating string of length L using techniques of plane geometry. Any interval in the real number line can be divided into n equal subintervals using compass and rule, as shown below for $n = 5$ and the interval $[a, b]$.

123

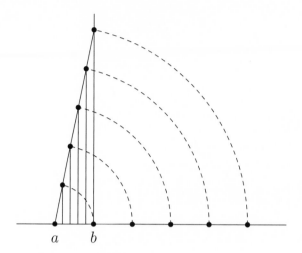

$$a \qquad b$$

If $\frac{n}{m} \geq 1$, its rational interval is obtained with the strings fundamental frequency by fretting the string at distance $\frac{m}{n} \cdot L \ (\leq L)$ from one end.

The intervals of equal temperament, however, were not so accessible before the development of relatively modern techniques. For example the semitone's ratio of $2^{1/12}$ would necessitate, as we have seen, finding the distance $2^{-1/12}L$ - a technique not accessible to ancient mathematicians.

Unique Factorization of Positive Rational Numbers. The following theorem about factorization in $\mathbb{Q}^+$ follows from the analogous theorem about $\mathbb{Z}^+$ from Chapter 8.

THEOREM. *Let* $x \in \mathbb{Q}^+$. *Then* x *can be factored as*

$$x = p_1^{\alpha_1} p_2^{\alpha_2} \cdots p_r^{\alpha_r}$$

where $r \geq 0$, $p_1, p_2, \ldots, p_r$ *are distinct primes, and* $\alpha_1, \alpha_2, \ldots, \alpha_r \in \mathbb{Z}, \neq 0$. *Moreover, this factorization is unique, meaning that if* $x = q_1^{\beta_1} q_2^{\beta_2} \cdots q_t^{\beta_t}$ *is another such factorization, then* $t = r$ *and after rearranging we have* $p_1 = q_1, p_2 = q_2, \ldots, p_r = q_r$.

Note that this statement differs from the analogous theorem about $\mathbb{Z}$ in that it allows the exponents $\alpha_1, \ldots, \alpha_r$ to be <u>non-zero</u> integers, not just positive ones. The proof of this theorem will be an exercise.

Given $x = p_1^{\alpha_1} \cdots p_r^{\alpha_r}$ as in the theorem, we may, without loss of generality, assume that $\alpha_1, \ldots, \alpha_i$ are positive and $\alpha_{i+1}, \ldots, \alpha_r$ are negative. Set

$s = r - i$, and let $\beta_j = -\alpha_{i+j}$ and $q_j = p_{i+j}$ for $j = 1, \ldots, s$. We have

$$x = \frac{p_1^{\alpha_1} p_2^{\alpha_2} \cdots p_i^{\alpha_i}}{q_1^{\beta_1} q_2^{\beta_2} \cdots q_s^{\beta_s}}$$

with $p_1, \ldots, p_i, q_1, \ldots, q_s$ being distinct primes and $\alpha_1, \ldots, \alpha_i, \beta_1, \ldots, \beta_s$ <u>positive</u> integers. We can easily write an element of $\mathbb{Q}$ in this form provided we can find the prime factorization of its numerator and denominator. The fraction $x = \frac{1,222,452}{11,180,400}$ seems intractable, but a little work with small primes gives the factorizations $1{,}222{,}452 = 11 \cdot 7^3 \cdot 3^4 \cdot 2^2$, $11{,}180{,}400 = 11^3 \cdot 7 \cdot 5^2 \cdot 3 \cdot 2^4$. Thus, by cancellation, we have

$$x = \frac{7^2 \cdot 3^3}{11^2 \cdot 5^2 \cdot 2^2} \, .$$

We will seek to understand rational intervals by the configuration of prime numbers $p_1, \ldots, p_i, q_1, \ldots, q_s$ which appear in their factorization, as above. We will first focus on some just intervals which are less than an octave, comparing them to their keyboard approximations.

We begin considering some cases where the denominator is a power of 2, i.e., rational intervals having ratio $n/2^\beta$, where n is odd. In this case, the interval is the composition of the integral interval n with $-\beta$ octaves. For example:

Just Fifth. Consider the interval given by $\frac{3}{2} \in \mathbb{Q}^+$. This is the integral interval 3 lowered by 1 octave. We noted in Chapter 8 that the interval 3 is ≈ 1.96 cents sharp of the keyboard's octave plus a fifth. Hence $\frac{3}{2}$ is sharp of a keyboard fifth by this same amount. (Or we can calculate directly: $1200 \log_2 \frac{3}{2} \approx 701.96$. The keyboards fifth is 700 cents.) The rational interval given by $\frac{3}{2}$ is called the *just fifth*.

approximation of 3 (≈ 2 cents flat)   approximation of $\frac{3}{2}$ (≈ 2 cents flat)

Just Major Third. The interval $\frac{5}{4}$ is the integral interval 5 minus two octaves. Recall that 5 is about 14 cents less than the keyboard's two octaves plus a major third. Hence $\frac{5}{4}$ is the same amount flat of the keyboard major third, and is called the *just major third*.

approx. of 5   ($\approx$ 14 cents sharp)   approx. of $\frac{5}{4}$ ($\approx$ 14 cents sharp)

Greater Whole Tone (Pythagorean Whole Tone). Since 3 is approximately one octave plus a fifth, the interval $\frac{9}{8}$ is twice that, lowered by three octaves: $\frac{9}{8} = (\frac{3}{2})^2 \cdot \frac{1}{2}$. This gives something close to the keyboard's step. The calculation $1200 \log_2 \frac{9}{8} \approx 203.91$ shows that this just interval is about 4 cents sharp of a step. We refrain from calling this interval the "just step" or "just whole tone" because we will soon encounter another just interval that is well approximated by the keyboard's one step. Instead, we will refer to this interval as the *greater whole tone.* It is also called the *Pythagorean whole tone,* for a reason that will be given in Chapter 12.

Now we will investigate some intervals having ratio $n/3^\beta$, where n is not divisible by 3.

Just Fourth. The most basic of these is the interval given by the ratio $\frac{4}{3}$. Note that this interval, call it I, is complimentary to the just fifth, since $\frac{4}{3} \cdot \frac{3}{2} = 2$. This says I is given additively as one octave minus a just fifth, which means it is about 2 cents flat of a keyboard fourth. We call I the *just fourth.*

approximation of $\frac{4}{3}$ ($\approx$ 2 cents sharp)

Lesser Whole Tone. The ratio $\frac{10}{9}$ gives another interval approximated by the keyboard step. We have $1200 \log_2 \frac{10}{9} \approx 182.40$, showing this interval to be about 18 cents flat of the keyboard's step. This interval will be called the *lesser whole tone.* Observe that the keyboard's step lies between the lesser and greater whole tones, closer to the latter, as indicated on the scale of cents below.

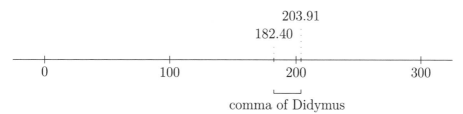

comma of Didymus

The interval between the lesser and greater whole tones has a ratio of $\frac{9}{8} \div \frac{10}{9} = \frac{81}{80}$ which is measured in cents by $1200 \log_2 \frac{81}{80} \approx 21.50$. This is called the *comma of Didymus,* named after the Greek music theorist Didymus the Musician (1st century AD).

Just Major Sixth. The fraction $\frac{5}{3}$ gives us an interval ≈ 884.36 measured in cents. Since it is only about 16 cents flat of the keyboard major sixth, we call it the *just major sixth.*

approximation of $\frac{5}{3}$ (≈ 16 cents sharp)

There are at least two common just intervals whose denominators involve the prime number 5.

Just Minor Third. By virtue of the equality $\frac{3}{2} \div \frac{5}{4} = \frac{6}{5}$, the ratio $\frac{6}{5}$ gives the interval I "between" the just major third and the just fifth, i.e., I is (additively) a just fifth minus a just major third. The cents measurement of $\frac{6}{5}$ is $1200 \log_2 \frac{6}{5} \approx 315.64$, about 16 cents sharp of the keyboard's minor third. We call it the *just minor third.*

approximation of $\frac{6}{5}$ (≈ 16 cents flat)

Just Semitone. We consider the fraction $\frac{16}{15} = \frac{2^3}{3 \cdot 5}$. By virtue of the fact that it has a larger numerator and denominator than any of those previously discussed, it gives an interval that might be considered "less just", and which one might expect to be less consonant. It is also the first ratio we have listed whose denominator involves more than one prime. We have $1200 \log_2 \frac{16}{15} \approx 111.73$, placing this interval about 12 cents sharp of the keyboard semitone.

It is called the *just semitone.*

approximation of $\frac{16}{15}$ (≈ 12 cents flat)

Septimal Intervals. All the just intervals above involve only the primes 2, 3, and 5. (According to a definition that will be given in the next chapter, these are *5-limit intervals.*) The prime 7 introduces us to still more just intervals, and these intervals are not so well approximated by 12-tone equal temperament. Three examples are the *septimal minor seventh,* with ratio $\frac{7}{4}$, its compliment the *septimal whole tone,* with ratio $\frac{8}{7}$, and the *septimal minor third,* with ratio $\frac{7}{6}$. These intervals are sufficiently far away from keyboard notes as to impart a texture that is sometimes called "blue", or "soulful", to music which employs them.

approximation of $\frac{7}{4}$ (≈ 31 cents sharp)   approximation of $\frac{8}{7}$ (≈ 31 cents flat)

approximation of $\frac{7}{6}$ (≈ 33 cents sharp)

Higher Primes. There is, in theory, an infinite list of higher primes to consider (the infinitude of the set of primes will appear as an exercise), but in practice there is a limit to the audible range of an interval. The human ear is able to listen to ratios up to about 1000, so there are indeed many audible possibilities. Although the primes > 7 may be considered remote, they can contribute intervals which have legitimate uses in music. These intervals, unnamed for the most part, will be referred to as "exotic". We often describe them by using the prefixes sub- and super- before the names of keyboard intervals.

An example is the exotic tritone, with ratio $\frac{11}{8}$. The fact $1200 \log_2 \frac{11}{8} \approx 551.32$ shows this interval to be almost halfway between the keyboard's fourth and tritone. Another is the exotic super-minor sixth given by $\frac{13}{8}$.

It is about 41 cents sharp of the keyboard's minor sixth, according to $1200 \log_2 \frac{13}{8} \approx 840.53$. These intervals are quite strange to the ear.

By contrast, the next two primes 17 and 19 give near-keyboard intervals as follows: A super-semitone is given by $\frac{17}{16}$, which is only about 5 cents sharp of the keyboard's semitone, and a sub-minor third is given by $\frac{19}{16}$, only 2 cents flat of the keyboard's minor third. Note that these rational intervals are better approximated by the keyboard than the just semitone and the just minor third.

The Comma of Pythagoras. The Greek mathematician Pythagoras (c. 540-510 B.C.) believed that the perfection of the (3 : 2) fifth (what we now call the just fifth) symbolized the perfection of the universe. Hence the tuning of the scale to achieve just fifths is called *Pythagorean tuning*. Pythagoras discovered that the iteration of twelve just fifths is almost the same as the iteration of seven octaves. This is demonstrated by:

$$\left(\frac{3}{2}\right)^{12} = \frac{3^{12}}{2^{12}} = \frac{531441}{4096} \approx 129.75\,,$$

$$2^7 = 128\,.$$

The interval between these is

$$\frac{\left(\frac{3}{2}\right)^{12}}{2^7} = \frac{3^{12}}{2^{19}} = \frac{531441}{524228} \approx 1.01364\,,$$

which is measured in cents by

$$1200 \log_2\left(\frac{3^{12}}{2^{19}}\right) \approx 23.46\,.$$

It is called the *comma of Pythagoras*.

This comma is the discrepancy we would get if we were to try to tune up the 12-note scale with just fifths. We know that the tempered (keyboard) fifth, iterated twelve times, gives us seven octaves. Thus if we let the circle represent all intervals (additively) modulo 7 octaves, then a fifth will be 1/12-th of the circle. Placing C at the top, we have the following clock.

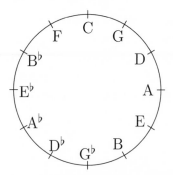

12-octave clock with tempered fifths

If we plot the 7-octave circle of fifths using just fifths, the twelve intervals add up to slightly more than one rotation, wrapping around the clock and ending up clockwise of the 12 o'clock position by precisely the comma of Pythagoras, as shown below. Thus the tuning of C would be problematic.

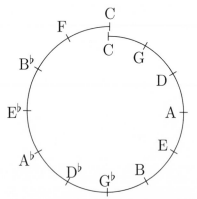

7-octave clock with just fifths

This small but non-negligible interval, not quite a quarter of a semitone, was greatly disturbing to Pythagoras.

Irrationality of Equally-Tempered Intervals. We will now show that all intervals between notes of the equally tempered scale, excepting iterations of the octave, are irrational, that is, they correspond to ratios which are irrational numbers, i.e., lie outside of $\mathbb{Q}$. In fact, this holds even in non-standard equally tempered scales.

THEOREM. *Let I be an interval between two notes in the chromatic n-scale. If I is not the iteration of octaves (i.e., the ratio corresponding to I is not a power of 2), then I is an irrational interval.*

Proof. Suppose I has ratio $x \in \mathbb{Q}^+$. The modular chromatic interval given by I, which lies in $\mathbb{Z}_n$, has finite order, which says that n iterations of I gives k octaves, for some positive integer n and some integer k. This says that $x^n = 2^k$. We know that x possesses a unique factorization $x = p_1^{\alpha_1} p_2^{\alpha_2} \cdots p_r^{\alpha_r}$ where $r \geq 0$, $p_1, p_2, \ldots, p_r$ are distinct primes, and $\alpha_1, \alpha_2, \ldots, \alpha_r \in \mathbb{Z}, \neq 0$. Thus we have

$$x^n = (p_1^{\alpha_1} p_2^{\alpha_2} \cdots p_r^{\alpha_r})^n = p_1^{n\alpha_1} p_2^{n\alpha_2} \cdots p_r^{n\alpha_r} = 2^k \,.$$

The uniqueness of this expression says that 2 is the only prime in the set of primes $\{p_1, \ldots, p_r\}$. Therefore $r = 1$ and $p_1 = 2$ (unless $k = 0$, in which case I is the unison interval). Hence $x = 2^{\alpha_1}$, which says I is an iteration of octaves. $\qquad\square$

This tells us that none of the intervals in any equally-tempered scale, save multi-octaves, are just, and suggests that none should be considered perfectly consonant. However, we have seen that the just intervals involving small powers of the primes 2, 3, and 5 have fairly close approximations in the 12-chromatic scale. For example, we have seen that the tempered fifth closely approximates $\frac{3}{2}$, and the tempered major third gives a fair approximation of $\frac{5}{4}$. This likely explains why the 12-chromatic scale gained acceptance. In the next chapter we will present some historical alternate methods of tuning the scale in unequal temperament designed to render some just intervals with precision, and discuss the advantages and limitations of such scales.

Justly Tuned Chords. We now observe that each rational interval is the interval between two harmonics of a sustained tone. Namely the interval ratio $n : m$, for $m, n \in \mathbb{Z}^+$, is the interval from the m-th to the n-th harmonic. Moreover the harmonic series contains "just" representations of most of the chords we discussed in Chapter 3.

A chord can be represented, with specified voicing, by writing a sequence of positive ratios $n_1 : n_2 : \cdots : n_k$. This means the chord has k pitches and the ratio between the i-th and the $(i + 1)$-st pitch is n_i. If the positive numbers $n_1, \ldots, n_k$ are all "small" integers ("small" being undefined) we say the chord is *justly tuned*. The smaller the integers in a chord's ratios, the more "harmonious", or consonant, it sounds. Chords whose ratios are not, or cannot be approximated by, small integers will sound "clashing", or dissonant.

Consider first the major chord. A just rendition of it comprises harmonics 4, 5, and 6, i.e., the chord given by the ratios $4 : 5 : 6$. Note that its third and fifth are a just major third and a just fifth, respectively, above its root, and that the interval between its third and fifth is a just minor third. The same chord written with doubled root in the "tenth voicing" (meaning the third is a tenth above the lowest root) can be realized as $2 : 3 : 4 : 5$. The keyboard approximations of these harmonics for F_2 are written below in small noteheads.

harmonics 4,5,6 of F_2 harmonics 2,3,4,5 of F_2

The presence of this chord in the lower harmonics surely explains why the chord is so pleasing and so basic in music.

Just renderings of this and other chords discussed in Chapter 3 appear "early" in the overtone series as follows:

major triad	$4 : 5 : 6$
seventh	$4 : 5 : 6 : 7$
half-diminished seventh	$5 : 6 : 7 : 9$
minor triad	$10 : 12 : 15$
minor seventh	$10 : 12 : 15 : 18$
major seventh	$8 : 10 : 12 : 15$

Obviously these tunings cannot be achieved on a normal keyboard. However with the human voice and with certain instruments, such as the violin, a continuum of pitch is available so that the ear of the musician fine-tunes the pitch. In these situations the singer/instrumentalist may be drawn toward the more natural just tuning over the imperfection (and irrationality) of equal temperament.

One tone that may sound annoyingly flat to some musicians is the septimal seventh that appears in the just seventh chord listed above. As we saw, it lies 31 cents below its keyboard approximation. However, it produces a seventh chord that is laser-like in its perfect consonance. This low seventh is often heard in blues, some jazz, and some *a cappella* vocal styles such as barbershop. A less consonant tuning of the seventh chord is given by $20 : 25 : 30 : 36$. Here the interval from root to seventh is $9 : 5$, an interval which is called the *just minor seventh* (as opposed to the septimal minor seventh).

The harmonic (overtone) series also explains more complicated harmonies such as those found in jazz. For example, the type of ninth chord shown below has the just tuning $4 : 5 : 6 : 7 : 9$.

Another example occurs in George Gershwin's *Rhapsody in Blue* as the final chord of this famous passage[1]:

Molto stentando

The striking six-note chord at the end can be tuned justly as $2 : 3 : 5 : 7 : 9 : 11$, whereupon all these notes occur as harmonics of $E^\flat_2$. Though the 7 and 11 are poorly approximated by equal temperament, the chord's primal appeal likely comes from its similarity to this just rendition.

The functionality of augmented and diminished seventh chords often plays on their property of having equal intervals, hence no discernable root.

---

[1] This excerpt also contains an m on n pattern as discussed in Chapter 8. The melodic (top) line repeats a sequence of eight notes: E_5, F_5, G_5, G_4, A_4, B_4, C_5, D_5. Beginning with the seventh measure, the notes are played in triplets, creating a 3 on 8 pattern. The double pattern is complete after $3 \times 8 = 24$ notes, which occupy measures 7-10, culminating in the caesura and the final jazz chord.

The theorem stated and proved earlier in this chapter shows that such equal partitions of the octave are unachievable in just intonation; completely symmetric chords can only be rendered using irrational temperament. Thus one might argue that augmented and full diminished chords are best rendered in equal temperament; perhaps they are even a *result* of equal temperament. This accounts for their unstable character.

Exercises

1. For each of these rational intervals, find the 12-chromatic interval which best approximates it, and calculate the error. Express the approximating interval by name (e.g., "minor third").

   (a) $\frac{5}{3}$ (b) $\frac{11}{10}$ (c) $\frac{19}{16}$ (d) $\frac{9}{7}$ (e) $\frac{5}{5}$

2. Give the prime factorizations of these rational numbers as $\dfrac{p_1^{\alpha_1} p_2^{\alpha_2} \cdots p_r^{\alpha_r}}{q_1^{\beta_1} q_2^{\beta_2} \cdots q_s^{\beta_s}}$ with

$$\{p_1, \ldots, p_r\} \cap \{q_1, \ldots, q_s\} = \emptyset,$$

writing the primes of the numerator and denominator in ascending order, as in $\frac{2^3 \cdot 5 \cdot 7^2}{3 \cdot 11^2 \cdot 13^3}$.

   (a) $\frac{150}{65}$ (b) $\frac{1000}{287}$ (c) $\frac{750}{980}$ (d) $\frac{512}{162}$ (e) $\frac{69}{289}$

3. Suppose $x \in \mathbb{Q}^+$ has the factorization $x = \dfrac{p_1^{\alpha_1} p_2^{\alpha_2} \cdots p_r^{\alpha_r}}{q_1^{\beta_1} q_2^{\beta_2} \cdots q_s^{\beta_s}}$ as in the previous exercise. What criterion about this factorization says x is an integer?

4. Give a direct proof that $\sqrt{2}$ is irrational. Interpret this as a statement about a musical interval.

5. Let p be a fixed prime. Verify that the set of rational numbers x whose prime factorization has the form $x = p_1^{\alpha_1} p_2^{\alpha_2} \cdots p_r^{\alpha_r}$ with $p_1, \ldots, p_r \le p$ forms a subgroup of $(\mathbb{Q}^+, \cdot)$. (Intonation which utilizes only interval ratios in this subgroup is called *p-limit tuning*.)

6. Show by multiplication and division in $\mathbb{Q}^+$ that:

   (a) a just major third plus a just minor third is a just fifth

   (b) a just fifth plus a septimal minor third is a just minor seventh

(c) a greater just whole tone plus a lesser just whole tone is a just major third

(d) the comma of Didymus plus one octave is two just fifths minus a lesser whole tone

(e) a just major third minus a just fourth is a just semitone downward

7. Show by comparing rational numbers that:

(a) three just major thirds is not an octave

(b) four just minor thirds is not an octave

(c) a just fifth plus two just semitones is not a just major sixth

(d) two just fourths is not a just minor seventh

(e) the difference between a just major third and a just minor third is not a just semitone

In each case above, calculate the difference as a rational interval ratio, with prime factorization, <u>and</u> calculate the difference in cents.

8. Prove that the (additive) measurement in octaves of a rational interval cannot be a rational number unless the interval is a multi-octave. (Hint: If interval ratio x is measured by $\frac{a}{b}$ octaves, we have $x = 2^{\frac{a}{b}}$. Use unique factorization in $\mathbb{Q}^+$.) Deduce that the measurement of such an interval in semitones or cents is irrational.

9. Find just tunings of these chords. The ratio should be reduced, meaning the integers involved have no common divisor other than 1.

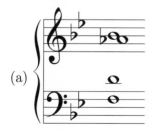
(a)

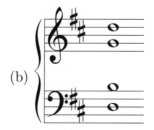
(b)

10. Find reduced just tunings of these chords using higher primes.

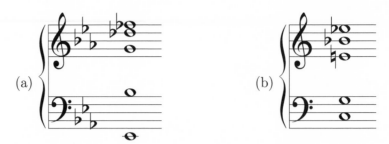

11. Suppose a vocal quartet sings a seventh chord on an *ah* vowel. The seventh chord is justly tuned, with septimal seventh, voiced bottom to top as fifth, seventh, root, third (within an octave), the root being middle C. The third formant of the *ah* vowel is centered at 2640 Hz. Suppose frequencies within a just major third of the center are amplified. Identify the harmonics from each of the four singers that are amplified. How many amplified frequencies are reinforced, i.e., appear in the overtone series of more than one of the singers?

Chapter 12

Tuning the Scale to Obtain Rational Intervals

We will now present some other traditional ways to tune the diatonic and chromatic scales in order to render certain intervals as just intervals. An understanding of the advantages and disadvantages of such scales will help to explain why the system of equal temperament eventually gained wide acceptance.

p-Limit Tuning. Given a prime number p, the subset of $\mathbb{Q}^+$ consisting of those rational numbers x whose prime factorization has the form $x = p_1^{\alpha_1} p_2^{\alpha_2} \cdots p_r^{\alpha_r}$ with $p_1, \ldots, p_r \leq p$ forms a subgroup of $(\mathbb{Q}^+, \cdot)$. (This will be an exercise.) We say that a scale or system of tuning uses *p-limit tuning* if all interval ratios between pitches lie in this subgroup.

The Pythagorean Scale. This scale, deriving its name from Pythagoras' high regard for the just fifth (ratio $3:2$), tunes the scale so that all intervals between scale tones are rational intervals involving only the primes 2 and 3. This means it has 3-limit tuning: all intervals between scale tones have ratios that can be expressed as $2^\alpha \cdot 3^\beta$. The Pythagorean scale arises from tuning each of the intervals in the upward sequence of scale tones

$$\hat{4} \to \hat{1} \to \hat{5} \to \hat{2} \to \hat{6} \to \hat{3} \to \hat{7}$$

to be $3:2$. Note that the diatonic notes occupy seven consecutive positions on the circle of fifths, starting at the 11 o'clock position and proceeding clockwise to the 5 o'clock position.

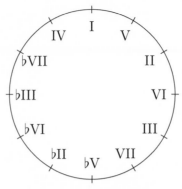

The Circle of Fifths

The Pythagorean scale simply tunes each of these fifths between diatonic notes to be just fifths.

We calculate the interval ratio from $\hat{1}$ to each scale tone within an octave by dividing. For example, the iteration $\hat{1} \to \hat{5} \to \hat{2}$ of two just fifths gives the interval $\frac{3}{2} \cdot \frac{3}{2} = \frac{9}{4}$. Since $2 < \frac{9}{4} < 4$, this interval lies between one and two octaves. So to get the scale tone $\hat{2}$ which is within one octave we divide by 2 to get $\frac{9}{4} \cdot \frac{1}{2} = \frac{9}{8}$. We recognize this interval as the Pythagorean whole tone (greater whole tone), whence the name.

In similar fashion, we calculate the interval between adjacent scale tones $\hat{1}$ and $\hat{3}$ to be

$$\left(\frac{3}{2}\right)^4 \cdot \left(\frac{1}{2}\right)^2 = \frac{3^4}{2^6} = \frac{81}{64}.$$

This interval, measured in cents is $1200 \log_2 \frac{81}{64} \approx 407.88$, about 8 cents sharp of the tempered major third, and about 22 cents sharp of the just major third.

The ratio of each of the scale tones to the scale tone $\hat{1}$ in the Pythagorean scale is given by this table:

scale tone :	$\hat{1}$	$\hat{2}$	$\hat{3}$	$\hat{4}$	$\hat{5}$	$\hat{6}$	$\hat{7}$	$\hat{8}$
ratio to $\hat{1}$:	$\frac{1}{1}$	$\frac{9}{8}$	$\frac{81}{64}$	$\frac{4}{3}$	$\frac{3}{2}$	$\frac{27}{16}$	$\frac{243}{128}$	$\frac{2}{1}$

Pythagorean diatonic scale

In this scale each of the five whole step intervals $\hat{1} \to \hat{2}$, $\hat{2} \to \hat{3}$, $\hat{4} \to \hat{5}$, $\hat{5} \to \hat{6}$, and $\hat{6} \to \hat{7}$ is two just fifths minus an octave, which is the Pythagorean whole tone (greater whole tone), whence the name. Both of the half-step intervals are given by the complicated ratio $\frac{256}{243} = \frac{2^8}{3^5}$, which Pythagoras called a *hemitone*. (The comparison of this interval with the tempered semitone and half the Pythagorean whole tone will appear as an exercise.) Thus the intervals between adjacent scale tones in the Pythagorean scale are given by:

$$\hat{1} \xrightarrow{9:8} \hat{2} \xrightarrow{9:8} \hat{3} \xrightarrow{256:243} \hat{4} \xrightarrow{9:8} \hat{5} \xrightarrow{9:8} \hat{6} \xrightarrow{9:8} \hat{7} \xrightarrow{256:243} \hat{8}$$

The Pythagorean scale can be extended to a chromatic scale by continuing to tune just fifths around the circle of fifths, but, as we have seen, the comma of Pythagoras prevents us from completing the circle using only just fifths. The comma is accommodated by allowing a "small" fifth between some two adjacent positions in the circle. This is often placed at one of the bottom clock positions, either between $\hat{7}$ and $b\hat{5}$ or between $b\hat{5}$ and $b\hat{2}$. Choosing the latter, we get:

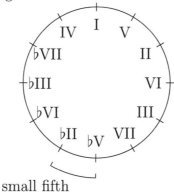

small fifth

A significant weakness of this scale is its poor representation of the major third as $\frac{81}{64}$, two Pythagorean whole tones. This ratio is even greater than the tempered major third, and is sharp of the just major third by precisely the comma of Didymus (exercise). We will call it the *Pythagorean major third.* The sharpness of this interval is easily perceived, and the dissonance heard in the major triads I, IV, and V when played in Pythagorean tuning render this system unacceptable for music in which a high level of consonance is desired.

The Just Intonation Scale. This scale employs 5-limit tuning in such a way that the diatonic major triads I, IV, and V are justly tuned, meaning that when these chords are voiced within an octave in root position, the ratios of root, third, and fifth are 4 : 5 : 6. In the key of C, this means the C, F, and G major triads will enjoy the consonance of just intonation.

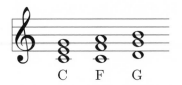

This is enough to define a tuning for each diatonic scale note, since each diatonic note is used in at least one of these three chords. The justness of the tonic triad I dictates $\hat{1} \to \hat{3}$ gives $\frac{5}{4}$ and $\hat{1} \to \hat{5}$ gives $\frac{3}{2}$. The justness of V says that $\hat{5} \to \hat{7}$ gives $\frac{5}{4}$, hence $\hat{1} \to \hat{7}$ is $\frac{3}{2} \cdot \frac{5}{4} = \frac{15}{8}$, and that $\hat{5} \to \hat{2}$ is $\frac{3}{4}$ (being downward a just fourth), hence $\hat{1} \to \hat{2}$ is $\frac{3}{2} \cdot \frac{3}{4} = \frac{9}{8}$, which is the greater whole tone. To effect the justness of IV, we deduce in similar fashion that the ratios of $\hat{4}$ and $\hat{6}$ to $\hat{1}$ must be $\frac{4}{3}$ and $\frac{5}{3}$, respectively. Thus the ratios of scale tones to $\hat{1}$ in the just intonation scale are given by:

scale tone :	$\hat{1}$	$\hat{2}$	$\hat{3}$	$\hat{4}$	$\hat{5}$	$\hat{6}$	$\hat{7}$	$\hat{8}$
ratio to $\hat{1}$:	$\frac{1}{1}$	$\frac{9}{8}$	$\frac{5}{4}$	$\frac{4}{3}$	$\frac{3}{2}$	$\frac{5}{3}$	$\frac{15}{8}$	$\frac{2}{1}$

Just intonation diatonic scale

Note the more consonant intervals with $\hat{1}$ given by scale notes $\hat{3}$, $\hat{6}$, and $\hat{7}$ over those of the Pythagorean scale.

In the just intonation scale the greater whole tone appears as the interval $\hat{1} \to \hat{2}$, $\hat{4} \to \hat{5}$, and $\hat{6} \to \hat{7}$, while $\hat{2} \to \hat{3}$ and $\hat{5} \to \hat{6}$ are the lesser whole tone. Both $\hat{3} \to \hat{4}$ and $\hat{7} \to \hat{8}$ are the just semitone. The intervals between adjacent scale tones in the just intonation scale are as follows:

$$\hat{1} \xrightarrow{9:8} \hat{2} \xrightarrow{10:9} \hat{3} \xrightarrow{16:15} \hat{4} \xrightarrow{9:8} \hat{5} \xrightarrow{10:9} \hat{6} \xrightarrow{9:8} \hat{7} \xrightarrow{16:15} \hat{8}$$

In addition to giving justly tuned major triads I, IV, and V, the just intonation scale gives justly tuned minor triads IIIm and VIm, and justly tuned minor sevenths IIIm^7 and VIm^7. (Recall that the minor triad in root position, voiced within an octave, is justly tuned as $10 : 12 : 15$ and the minor seventh is justly tuned as $10 : 12 : 15 : 18$.)

The just intonation scale is extended to a chromatic scale in such a way as to render certain other triads in just intonation, as follows.

1. $\flat\hat{6}$ and $\flat\hat{3}$ are tuned so that $\flat$VI is justly tuned. This places $\flat\hat{6}$ a just major third below $\flat\hat{8}$ and $\flat\hat{3}$ a just minor third above $\hat{1}$.

2. $\flat\hat{7}$ is tuned a just minor third above $\hat{5}$. This makes $\flat$III a justly tuned major triad.

3. $\flat\hat{2} = \sharp\hat{1}$ is tuned so that VI is justly tuned.

4. $\flat\hat{5} = \sharp\hat{4}$ is tuned to be a just fourth below $\hat{7}$. This makes VIIm a justly tuned minor triad.

With this chromatic scale many, but not all, of the major triads, minor triads, and minor sevenths are justly tuned. For example, Im^7 and IVm^7 are just, but the major triads II and III are both bad, the former having a flat fifth and the latter having a sharp third. This, unfortunately, precludes well-tuned chords in any extensive circle-of-fifths root movement.

Since the just intonation scale utilizes 5-limit tuning, there are no septimal intervals, hence no septimal seventh chords. Several of the seventh chords, such as I^7, have the tuning obtained by placing the seventh a just minor third (ratio $\frac{6}{5}$) above the fifth. This gives a seventh tuned as $20 : 25 : 30 : 36$, which is decidedly less consonant than the septimal seventh chord $4 : 5 : 6 : 7$. Even worse, the most needed seventh in conventional harmony, V^7, is even less consonant, since the interval $\hat{2} \rightarrow \hat{4}$ is not even a just minor third. An easy exercise in arithmetic shows this chord has the tuning $36 : 45 : 54 : 64$.

The Classical Mean-Tone Scale. The acceptance of thirds into Western music, which occurred in the 14th and 15th centuries, brought the need for tuning which goes beyond the 3-limit. Certain compromises were introduced which detuned fifths in order to improve the sound of thirds. Such scales are called *mean-tone* scales. We will discuss the one which became most common, called the *classical mean-tone scale;* henceforth this is what we will mean when we use the term "mean-tone scale".

Unlike the Pythagorean and just intonation scales, the mean-tone scale allows some irrational intervals. All of its rational intervals lie in the subgroup of $\mathbb{Q}^+$ consisting of those elements whose prime factorization involves only 2 and 5.

The idea of the mean-tone scale is to shrink the fifths around the clock equally so that the major third spanning four clock positions (modulo octave) is the just major third, having ratio $5 : 4$. One way to calculate the ratio r of such a fifth is to note that 4 iterations of this interval should equal 2 octaves plus a just major third, i.e.,

$$x^4 = 4 \cdot \frac{5}{4} = 5,$$

therefore $x = \sqrt[4]{5} = 5^{\frac{1}{4}} \approx 1.49535$.

(Note that the closeness of this ratio, ≈ 1.49535, to $1.5 = \frac{3}{2}$.) This is an irrational interval (exercise) whose measurement in cents is calculated by

$$1200 \log_2 \sqrt[4]{5} = 1200 \log_2 5^{\frac{1}{4}} = \frac{1200}{4} \log_2 5 = 300 \log_2 5 \approx 696.58 \,.$$

Thus the *mean-tone fifth* lies about 3 cents flat of the tempered fifth and about 5 cents flat of the just fifth – tolerably close.

However, as with the Pythagorean scale, there must be a comma in the circle. The problem is that three just major thirds do not constitute an octave, as seen by

$$\left(\frac{5}{4}\right)^3 = \frac{125}{64} < \frac{128}{64} = 2 \,.$$

Hence if we tune fifths around the clock so that every four consecutive clock positions equals (modulo octave) a just major third, then the twelfth position does not coincide with the starting point, being flat by the interval ratio $2/(\frac{125}{64}) = \frac{128}{125}$, which is about 41 cents. Therefore a "large fifth" is placed somewhere on the lower left side of the clock, usually located so that it does not occur between diatonic scale tones. For example, it could be placed between the 8 and 9 o'clock positions, as depicted below.

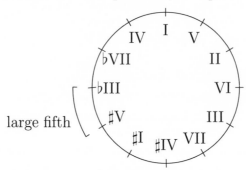

The large fifth which appears in the mean-tone chromatic scale, lying about two fifths of a semitone sharp of the just fifth or tempered fifth, was long ago dubbed the *wolf fifth*, after the animal's howl.

With the wolf fifth placed away from the diatonic clock positions, each diatonic whole tone equals two mean-tone fifths minus an octave, which has ratio $(\sqrt[4]{5})^2/2 = \sqrt{5}/2$, calculated in cents by $1200 \log_2(\sqrt{5}/2) \approx 193.157$, about 7 cents flat of the tempered step. We can calculate the interval between I and each of the scale tones. For example, the interval between scale tones I and VI is three mean-tone fifths minus an octave, and has ratio $5^{3/4}/2$.

Here is a table of such ratios.

scale tone :	$\hat{1}$	$\hat{2}$	$\hat{3}$	$\hat{4}$	$\hat{5}$	$\hat{6}$	$\hat{7}$	$\hat{8}$
ratio to I :	$\frac{1}{1}$	$\frac{\sqrt{5}}{2}$	$\frac{5}{4}$	$\frac{2}{5^{\frac{1}{4}}}$	$\frac{5^{\frac{1}{4}}}{1}$	$\frac{5^{\frac{3}{4}}}{2}$	$\frac{5^{\frac{5}{4}}}{4}$	$\frac{2}{1}$

mean-tone diatonic scale

Drawbacks of Unequal Temperament. Each of the three scales discussed in this chapter has certain advantages. The Pythagorean scale gives a just fifth almost always. The just intonation scale gives many perfectly tuned chords. The mean-tone scale, with the comma placed as above, gives tolerably tuned major triads on each of the diatonic roots except VII, and even this triad would be well-tuned if we rotated the comma one position clockwise. (Why?)

One obvious drawback of each of these systems is that some intervals are poorly tuned. This Pythagorean scale gives poor thirds, and one weak fifth. The just intonation scale renders the major triads II and III with less-than-desirable tuning. The mean-tone scale has one very bad fifth.

But a more serious problem with these scales is their asymmetry with respect to the choice of key. A keyboard instrument cannot be conveniently retuned between songs, or in the middle of a piece that changes key. If the keyboard is tuned to the just intonation scale in the key of C, a song in D has serious problems because the tonic triad is distractingly out of tune. This is what fed the gradual adoption of equal temperament. In the equally tempered scale, one has to accept sharp thirds and sevenths, but all chords of the same type are tuned precisely the same, regardless of their root relative to the key. While this imperfect tuning was a bitter pill to swallow, it allowed composers and performers to use extensive harmonic variety and freely modulate from one key to another. A great deal of 19th and 20th century music is deeply entrenched in this liberation.

In the first half of the 18th century J. S. Bach produced a bold demonstration of equal temperament[1] by producing his famous *Well-Tempered Clavier,* a collection of 48 preludes and fugues, assembled in two parts, each part containing 24 pieces representing each of the major and minor keys. Another example of a composition which exploits this harmonic emancipation is Franz Listz's classic piano piece *Liebestraum* (19th century) which

---

[1]Actually, music historians disagree as to whether Bach was actually touting equal temperament or some other system quite close to equal temperament.

extensively traverses the circle of fifths, modulates several times, and uses every root note in the chromatic scale of its initial (and final) key, $A^\flat$.

Exercises

1. Give just tunings for each of these jazz chords by utilizing "exotic" primes, i.e., primes which are ≥ 7.

2. The Pythagorean scale's minor third is one greater whole tone plus one hemitone, called a *Pythagorean minor third.* Express it as a ratio and compare it, as ratios and in cents, to the tempered minor third and the just minor third.

3. Show that the interval between the just major third and the Pythagorean major third is the comma of Didymus. Explain why the mean-tone fifth is flat of the just by one-fourth of the comma of Didymus, and use this to recalculate the mean-tone fifth in cents.

4. Suppose the following passage is tuned so that if a note is a fifth or minor third, modulo octave, from a note in the previous chord, then that interval is just. Show that the final G will be sharp of the initial G by the comma of Didymus.

   (This example was presented in 1585 by the Venetian scholar G. B. Benedetti (1530-1590).)

5. Which major triads in the mean-tone scale have relatively good fifths but poor thirds? (Place the comma between the 8 and 9 o'clock po-

sitions.) How does mean-tone temperament render the minor third, compared with the just minor third?

6. Suppose these chords are in root position, voiced within an octave using the just intonation scale. Give the reduced ratio for each chord. Which of these chords will be "pleasing" when this is played in the just intonation scale? Define *pleasing* to mean it uses only integers ≤ 20 when expressed as a reduced ratio.

    (a) VIm   (b) III   (c) IV^{+9} (d) $\flat II^{7}$ (e) V^{6}

7. Identify those fifths which in the just intonation chromatic scale's circle of fifths are not just fifths $\left(\frac{3}{2}\right)$, and express each of these "imperfect" fifths as a reduced ratio of integers $n_1 : n_2$.

8. Assume we have tuned the Pythagorean chromatic scale with the comma placed between VII and $\flat$V. Certain of the major triads with perfect (i.e., just) fifths have better thirds by virtue of the fact that the third lies across the comma from the root and fifth. Calculate the difference of this third from the just major third in cents and identify by Roman numeral which major triads possess this property.

Bibliography

[1] G. Assayag, H. G. Feichtinger, and J. F. Rodrigues (eds.), *Mathematics and Music: A Diderot Mathematical Forum*, Springer-Verlag, 1997.

[2] David J. Benson, *Music: A Mathematical Offering*, Cambridge University Press, 2007.

[3] David Cope, *New Music Composition*, Schirmer Books, New York, 1977.

[4] Trudi Hammel Garland and Charity Vaughn Kahn, *Math and Music: Harmonious Connections*, Dale Seymour Publications, 1995.

[5] Leon Harkleroad, *The Math Behind the Music*, Cambridge University Press, 2007.

[6] Sir James Jeans, *Science and Music*, Cambridge University Press, 1937, Reprinted by Dover, 1968.

[7] Thomas D. Rossing, *The Science of Sound*, second ed., Addison Wesley, 1990.

[8] Rex Wexler and Bill Gannon, *The Story of Harmony*, Justonic Tuning Inc., 1997.

Index